December 1, 2014

To Paul and Julie,

with much love and with thanksgiving to our Lord for both of you!

Paul, I must tell you that your words of encouragement have been very meaningful to me through the years. You have refreshed my spirit more than you know.

May our Savior's great Hand of blessing be upon both of you!

Lord

PRAISE FOR
Rulers: Gospel and Government

"In an age of culture wars, bitter partisanship, and slogan-soaked theology, there are few issues of greater importance if we are to stem the tide of Christian ghettoization and irrelevance. It is so encouraging to read the efforts of these individuals who work with integrity and conviction, but below the media radar, in the corridors of power. This book is a timely challenge to those who complacently hurl their criticisms (and even abuse) from the security of the political sidelines or church pulpits. I hope and pray that many will now quietly take up the same burden as Chuck and his colleagues."

—Mark Meynell, European Programme Director,
Langham Partnership and Chaplain to
HM Treasury and Revenue & Customs, Westminster, London

"Chuck Garriott's compilation of essays is a unique guidepost for men and women seeking to impact those who make decisions in the halls of power. He rightfully reminds us that Christ should be ever-present for those with decision-making responsibilities. I know you will find Chuck's work an inspiration as I did."

—Dan Boren, former U.S. Representative,
D-OK, 2nd District

"Charles Garriott's insight grows from his friendship with governors, senators, White House officials, and political leaders worldwide. He spends his days discreetly encouraging office holders and their staffs spiritually, while recruiting others to pray for them. I enthusiastically recommend *Rulers*. Its stories and reflections, penned by a former HUD secretary and others, will equip ordinary Christians to strengthen their country by spiritually supporting its leaders."

—Steven Estes, pastor, author, conference speaker

"It is great encouragement to read of those who take with a holy seriousness their calling to extend the incarnation, that is, to be what C. S. Lewis called "little Christs," in a city where large personalities dominate. It gives hope to hear from those who work in Washington whose interior lives are shaped by belonging to Christ before every other loyalty. Thank the Lord for Chuck Garriott and the work of Ministry to State."

—Joseph (Skip) Ryan, Redeemer Seminary

"*Rulers: Gospel and Government* is an inspiring and instructive book that defines and clarifies the critical relationship between Christianity and government. The authors relate a rich variety of approaches that depict their experiences in the resolution of the tension that often underlies attempts to guide statecraft with the gospel. These articles provide a powerful testimony and encouragement to those, like me, who are searching and striving for ways to bring godliness into the conduct of government. I thank Charles Garriott and all the authors for this book. It is a remarkable and noteworthy contribution to the search for good governance in our time and in future generations as well."

—Ezra Suruma, former Minister of Finance, Planning and Economic Development, Uganda

"As I read *Rulers* I could not help but meditate on the sovereign rule of God. From the humble narratives to the powerful application, this book has changed the way I think and pray for rulers. Read this book and see the power of Christ's reign in redeeming rulers. You will pray differently."

—Mark Davis, Parks Cities Presbyterian Church, Dallas

"We are told to pray for those in authority. If we obey that command, we will grow in sympathy for those called to government service. Chuck Garriott has developed that sympathy through his own ministry of prayer and pastoral service to political leaders. Now he has assembled a team of like-minded servants who practice the Lordship of Christ over all areas of life, including civil government. Like Daniel of an earlier era, these servants carry that Lordship into the political realm, where it is so much needed."

—Russ Pulliam, *Indianapolis Star*

RULERS

GOSPEL AND GOVERNMENT

Edited by

Charles M. Garriott

Riott

Washington D.C.

RIOTT
Washington D.C.

Rulers: Gospel and Government

Interior design by Jeffrey M. Hall, www.iongdw.com

Cover designed by Christopher Tobias, tobiasdesign.com

ISBN: 978-0-9762004-4-4

RELIGION/SPIRITUAL

Printed in the United States of America

First Printing 2014

May all the kings of the earth praise you, LORD,
when they hear the words of your mouth.
May they sing of the ways of the LORD,
for the glory of the LORD IS GREAT.

—King David, 1010-970 B.C.

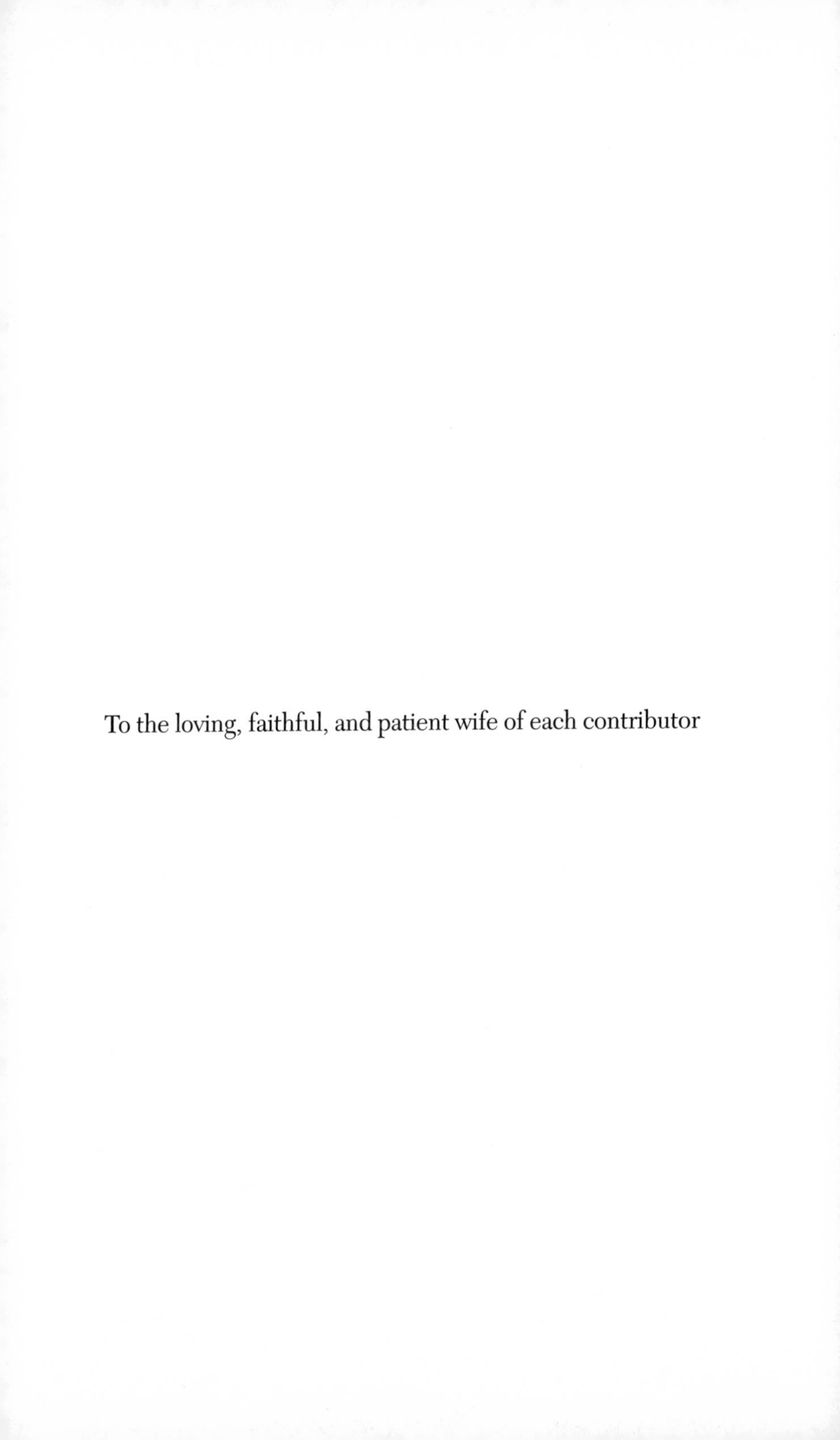

To the loving, faithful, and patient wife of each contributor

CONTENTS

BEFORE YOU BEGIN...

I have known Chuck Garriott, the director of Ministry to State (MTS), for decades. In that time, he always has impressed me as a man who is exceedingly comfortable in sharing Christ one-on-one. So I wasn't surprised when I learned that Chuck was organizing a one-on-one ministry that would reach leaders in government.

The whole idea behind Ministry to State is totally incongruent to "politics as usual." It builds relationships not to receive something, gain favor, push an agenda, glad-hand, or seek a vote; rather, it's about *giving*. And *caring* about individuals who know what it feels like to be used. What better way to shake gospel salt or shine Christ's light into America's political culture?!

Much time has passed since Chuck and his team laid the foundation for Ministry to State. That is why I especially enjoyed reading *Rulers: Gospel and Government*. As I perused its pages, I came to know the stories of remarkable men who have responded to God's call to get up day after day and head out humbly into the halls of power. Hearing their personal stories and struggles has helped me see how MTS leaders are men of prayer who respect confidences, hold fast to integrity, and provide godly counsel when asked. Whether a state or federal congressman or staff worker is "Blue" or "Red" is not the issue – making Jesus real is, then allowing the Holy Spirit to do the rest.

Rulers: Gospel and Government exposed me to the unseen work God is doing in our state assemblies, U.S. Congress, and local and federal agencies. Reading about the one-on-one encounters MTS leaders and friends have with government officials has given me a grassroots picture of what Ministry to State actually *does*. It has bolstered my hopes for the future of our country!

I hope you will feel the same after reading the small but significant book you hold in your hands. If you are interested in civil service or are studying political science, consider getting involved with Ministry to State. Pray for MTS. But whatever the take-away from this book, be encouraged. Be hopeful and heartened. God is on the move in our government, and He is far from finished with our nation.

—Joni Eareckson Tada
Joni and Friends International Disability Center
Spring 2014

PROLOGUE

Kings, rulers and kingdoms—and those who serve them—are rather common in Scripture. Egyptian pharaohs, Assyrian, Babylonian and Persian kings, and the many rulers of Israel and Judah dominate both Scripture and non-redemptive history. Libraries can hardly hold the countless volumes of books and dissertations that contain their stories. While forms of government in much of the world have shifted in more recent times to democracies and republics, in some ways what drives and characterizes rulers has not changed over the last four millennia. Regardless of the times, most seem to have a similar disease: too much self. Even the ones who start off well can fall into the same rut of arrogance, pride, boastfulness, and, most of all, failing to remember who is really King. Yes, there are exceptions, but not many.

The life-dominating media today remind us that little has changed in our modern and progressive times. True, some rulers in past and present centuries have been benevolent and thoughtful, but others are hardcore malevolent. And, as always, they don't rule alone. Myriads of advisors, secretaries, councils and scholars breathe in the fumes of power. They also have those who serve in their agencies—the bureaucrats. You might wonder who really is in charge. Yet, despite various opinions on their rule, service, accomplishments and failures, they have one thing in common: They are made in the image of God. This is the reason a desire to govern or rule exists in each of their hearts.

In some ways it is the distorted exercise of that divine stamp that causes the problem. Leaders' distorted desires and poor performances are a result of failed attempts to properly work out what it means for them to exist in God's image. Political parties make no difference in all this. For this reason, governmental leadership merits direct gospel influence and ministry. The church should engage with those in government as marred image bearers who need Christ.

This small work provides some examples of why and how the gospel can influence government. While not exhaustive, it gives a sense of what it looks like for the church to intentionally pursue those in government with the truths of the Scriptures. It is my hope that the essays by various contributors will help you not only better understand the potential that such ministries can have, but also motivate you at least to pray for such a needy bunch.

CHAPTER 1

CALLING

CHARLES M. GARRIOTT

As I write, Nelson Mandela lies in state in Pretoria, South Africa. Eighteen months after his release from prison in the spring of 1991, I landed in Johannesburg to visit my dying friend, Richard Morrison. A fast-moving cancer was ravaging his body, and Richard's battle would last only a few more weeks. The image of his suffering is as vivid in my mind now as if it were yesterday.

This was my first of many visits to a country that was on a new political course after years of oppression and racial tension. I had an insatiable appetite to learn the history and culture of this people and their land. I had little idea that my brief friendship with Richard and my experience in South Africa would significantly influence my future call and ministry.

In April of 1993, I returned to Johannesburg with my wife, Debby, and our four young children for a six-month sabbatical from my Oklahoma City pastorate. We moved into a rented home in north Johannesburg, bought a used four-door Belarus (Honda Civic), opened a bank account and enrolled our children in the government schools. We would live like most white South Africans: safely ensconced in a secure, walled-in home whose flowerbeds and trees were maintained by our Zulu gardener, Lovemoore. We worshiped at St. George's Church, where gracious parishioners welcomed the new non-Anglican family from the States. Some of these friends invited us to their homes for dinner and participated in our ministry forums and Bible studies. I felt privileged to spend time with friends like Jonathan Paton, the son of noted writer Alan Paton, and talk about God and life over lunch at the University of the Witwatersrand, where he taught.

During the sabbatical, I regularly drove thirty minutes into Soweto to spend time with Pastor Jake Mabaso[1] at his church. I entered the township to preach, attend a funeral, assist with leadership training or just enjoy the fellowship. Through his eyes and stories, I began to understand the impact of apartheid. My education would not have been complete without the friendship of Professor Graeme McLean, who introduced me to his African National Congress (ANC) friends from Oxford, Wilhelm and Malini Verwoerd. Wilhelm was the grandson of the architect of apartheid, Prime Minister Hendrick Verwoerd. After the 1994 election, Wilhelm would become a researcher for the Truth and Reconciliation Commission. His wife Malini would become a Member of Parliament and later serve as South African ambassador to Ireland.

During my six months in South Africa, violence and bloodshed overflowed in the townships surrounding Johannesburg and in Kwa Zulu-Natal. The tension between the ANC and Inkatha Freedom Party resulted in more than 14,000 deaths in the years leading up to the 1994 election. The *Johannesburg Star* reported that the morgues could not hold the hundreds of bodies taken there each week as a result of this brutality. The same was true for other regions of the country. Hours after arriving in Cape Town on the 25th of July to lecture at the Bible Institute of South Africa, a horrific attack took place at the Anglican Church near where I was staying.

In the midst of the service, four gunmen with grenades and automatic gunfire killed eleven worshippers and seriously injured fifty more. Several of my students witnessed this event known as the St. James Massacre.

These were tense times in a country in upheaval. No one knew if the conflict might erupt into a full scale civil war. But it never did. It was averted by the landmark 1994 election: one man, one vote. As a result, the Robben Island prisoner, Nelson Mandela, became president.

What circumstances had led to decades of oppressive policies and violence? The answer is complicated. Yet part of the responsibility lies with the church, especially the Dutch Reformed side of the ecclesiastical community, whose misinterpretation of Scripture provided a theology for the government's apartheid policy.[2]

By the time of South Africa's landmark 1994 elections, we had settled back in Oklahoma City. I would return annually for a couple of weeks to Cape Town to lecture at the Bible Institute, preach, and visit friends. The political violence that had dominated South Africa quieted. But in an odd way, it seemed to follow me.

Two and a half years after our return to the United States, I heard the horrific blast set off by Timothy McVeigh in downtown Oklahoma City. It was April, 19, 1995, and though I was miles away, it sounded dangerously close. Within a few days, I was at a secure site, ministering to affected family members who had lost loved ones. It reminded me of my post-trauma discussions with Cape Town students who had witnessed the St. James Massacre. Both experiences provided an opportunity to view government from a different perspective. In Oklahoma City, I saw government engage in a form of "mercy ministry" in a time of great violence. I witnessed how a government can impact its constituents in a time of need and how the faith of government leaders can impact policy significantly. This would ultimately influence my view of government and my call to ministry.

A few months after the last bombing memorial service in OKC, I began to lead a small group Bible study with a handful of men at the state capitol at the request of my good friend Robert Whittaker. I devoted a portion of each Wednesday to those who worked in the various divisions of the state government. As this Bible study and lunch grew, we moved to Governor Frank Keating's Large Conference Room to accommodate the fifty to seventy attendees. On occasion, Governor Keating attended and spoke about how Scripture had impacted his life. At other times Lieutenant Governor Mary Fallen prayed with us. During the legislative session, I met separately with Democratic and Republican members of both House and Senate for Bible study and prayer. On some occasions, these friends would sponsor legislative prayer breakfasts that met at the Oklahoma University Faculty House on North Lincoln Boulevard.

It was a unique season in my ministry as a pastor. I loved the church and the Oklahoma City community in which we ministered. It was and continues to be a great source of encouragement and blessing for me and my family. Yet I began to be haunted by the prospect that my calling was changing. I sensed that the privilege of pastoring a local church was coming to an end. I needed direction from God.

As I sought wisdom and direction regarding my calling, I led a study of the book of Genesis. I had difficulty grasping the extent of mankind's wickedness in the early chapters of Genesis—wickedness that had caused God deep grief in the time leading up to the flood. I wondered, "Just how bad could it have been in the days of Noah?" Scripture does not provide the details. Concurrently, I was reading Paul Johnson's *Modern Times*, a history of the twentieth century. Johnson's book presented an 800-page version of modern malevolence by those in power. He wrote about the 125 million people who had died at the hands of world leaders, including Vladimir Lenin, Joseph Stalin, Adolf Hitler, Pol Pot, Idi Amin, and Saddam Hussein. Their victims did not die from war, famine, natural disaster or disease, but from directives issued by the heads of states and the government bureaucracies that enforced them. This past century, Johnson argues, was one of the most evil and wicked in all of history.[3] How could our progressive and modern world unleash such animosity and hate? Perhaps only a modern world could engineer this apocalyptic outpouring of depravity. I was shocked and sobered to realize that the instigators were all world leaders who had convinced their ministers, secretaries, and military that murdering millions of citizens was a noble act that would improve society and the world.[4]

I also visited Hungary in the early 1990s, and saw firsthand the effects of forty-five years under an oppressive regime. I thought I had stepped back in time to the 1950s: cars and fashion were very dated. The now-broken Soviet Army was still an unwanted occupier. I sat at the dinner tables of friends who lived under constant scrutiny and were denied basic human rights and freedoms. Pastors were required to report to the communist office in town every week to document their activities of the previous week and disclose their plans for the coming week. People were regularly watched and threatened, and Communist Party officials maintained files on everyone. For the most part, only the elderly dared attend church; workers risked losing their jobs for attending religious services. Except for prayer, people were without hope for change. Yet change did come.

As I considered God's judgment in Genesis, Johnson's overview of the twentieth century, and my time in Hungary and South Africa, I wondered if God were grieving over the world in our generation. What was the role of the Christian community, the church, within a nation's geographic government centers? The church has been passive at times, or worse, an enabler of evil governance.[5] Segments of the Reformed church in South Africa had developed a theology that led to and supported apartheid.[6] Did we not do the same with slavery here in America? Much of the church did not speak up regarding these evils; a silent church enabled the abuse of men, women and children for generations. The church was equally silent when it came to the treatment of Native Americans. Even today there are cultural issues of injustice that the church does not know how to address.

Can the church be a gospel presence within government centers of our nation and world? If the church were more engaged, could it be more influential? While there is a place for Christian individuals and organizations to influence policy and laws according to their concerns, I became convinced that shaping policy would *not* be my calling. I was drawn by the need for those in the church to engage leaders and those who serve them on a *personal basis* for their benefit in the gospel. It is impossible to know, but I have wondered what might have been the consequences in Europe if noted pastor Dietrich Bonhoeffer had devoted his life to such a form of ministry—ministry that pursued heads of state, their ministers and bureaucrats with a specialized focus of the gospel through personal relationships. Naïve? Wishful thinking?

I had witnessed this to a degree at the state capitol in Oklahoma City, where a ministry had developed to the individual public servant. Yet it was problematic for me to engage in this form of ministry. I was not politically savvy, experienced, or naturally interested in spending my time in the political community. For me, it would be cross-cultural work in an unfamiliar environment; however, I had a strong sense that God was calling me to be more involved. I wanted to be a trustworthy steward of all he had given and follow this divine directive.

I knew that if God were calling me into this work that my church would need to buy into it as well. The church leadership would need to concur. No such evidence existed. In addition, my denomination, the Presbyterian Church in America (PCA), might not consider this a reasonable theater in which to engage—and for good reason.

The normal pastorate is all-consuming. The only reason I had invested any time at the Oklahoma state capitol was because I had been invited to lead a Bible study—an invitation that was not entirely attractive. My twenty-plus years as a pastor of a church of some two hundred and fifty souls consumed my life and schedule. I worked with a team of pastors that needed my attention. On Sundays, I preached twice in the morning, led a new member's class and often taught in the evening on the south side of Oklahoma City, where we were planting a new church. My week was full with staff and leadership meetings, men's Bible studies, and counseling sessions in addition to sermon and other teaching preparation. It was non-stop. In no way was I able to devote a large portion of a day each week to the state capitol. Yet I did. I began to understand the significance of spending time with those who worked in and influenced the state's seat of power. Would other church leaders see and do the same?

Second, people fear that interacting with those in government (whether elected officials or civil servants) is inherently political. Most are uncomfortable with a church and activities that seem partisan. That is, the church has no business mingling in the affairs of the state, including spending any regular time in ministry with the people who serve in a state or federal capital. It becomes too complicated for a local congregation and is believed best left alone. What church wants to look like a political movement? Not many in my ecclesiastical circles.

A third reason why a ministry to leaders and government workers might fail to get traction is because in certain ways, the church can be a passive, ingrown body. Some believers may embrace a false view that the Christian life is only defined by attendance in a quiet setting of worship. For pastors, success and sustainability are too easily measured by the size of your budget and the number on the roll. Sadly, a church of twenty-five people who had come to Christ through the new ministry, were growing spiritually, and were strategic in gospel transformation within their community, workplace, schools and government centers would impress few. The work to which I felt directed would call the church to develop a form of "smart ministry"[7]: interacting and developing meaningful relationships with specific parts of the community outside the church in the context of the gospel.

I knew after a season of prayer and discussion with Debby that my future at our church was tentative and going to change. I wanted to devote more time to encouraging the church to pursue an atypical model of outreach and ministry. But how?

I started with my congregation and its leadership. Over several months, I shared my thoughts with my elders. They were not thrilled with what I understood to be the changing nature of my calling, yet were supportive. They reluctantly agreed to let us stay under their auspices for an eighteen-month period while we moved to Washington, D.C., and explored the nature of this new ministry. Such a ministry would need to be headquartered in Washington. Debby and I knew that the move would be financially difficult and would greatly alter our family life. We subsequently found that relocating to Washington was far more expensive and challenging than anything we had experienced, including our time in South Africa. We also learned that when your sense of God's calling is clear, you can accept uncertainties and difficulties.

In the summer of 2003, we moved from a spacious five-bedroom home in north Oklahoma City into a two-bedroom apartment off Massachusetts Avenue in northwest D.C. Debby found a full-time job as a physical therapist, and our youngest child, Peter, enrolled in a high school in Maryland. Wide open skies and spacious suburbia were replaced with congested urban traffic and crowded living spaces. Life and home were redefined.

In the two years that followed, my prayer that this fledgling ministry would be ecclesiastically based was answered. Ministry to State (MTS) was christened and placed under the Presbyterian Church in America's Mission to North America. MTS would develop in three major theaters: Washington, D.C., domestic state capitals, and international capitals. We would engage those in government with the truths of the gospel. It would be a "smart ministry" where the gospel and its benefits are intentionally and winsomely taken into the work- or marketplace.

The Barna research group reminds us that passive ministry (one that attempts to draw people into a worship service) fails to reach a significant portion of Americans.[8] Nearly a hundred million Americans do not attend any form of worship within a six-month period, and are not interested in a church regardless of its denomination or style of worship. If nonbelievers are to be reached, outreach needs to be directed to where they live or work.

Therefore, smart ministry became an essential part of the calling and work. After moving to Washington, I developed relationships with congressional members and their staffs on Capitol Hill that expanded into Bible studies, prayer breakfasts, and dinner forums. To address certain themes with a biblical world and life view, I undertook writing and publishing projects that helped further the work. Friendships emerged with White House staff that included a member of the president's cabinet. In the international community, I met diplomats here in Washington or traveled to other countries, spending time with members of the Diet in Japan, members of the Assembly National in Port-au-Prince, Haiti, and lawmakers in Kampala, Uganda. Over the years, doors opened one after another and the network of friendships has continued to grow. We saw God provide needed support through generous commitments and gifts from friends, churches and foundations.

The ministry has a long way to go, but it is emerging. It is a good gospel effort and is accomplishing its design. My calling has changed, but I now understand its scope.

King David provides a glimpse of what it look likes when rulers are sensitive and responsive to the gospel in their work:

The God of Israel spoke,
the Rock of Israel said to me:
'When one rules over people in righteousness,
when he rules in the fear of God,
he is like the light of morning at sunrise
on a cloudless morning,
like the brightness after rain
that brings grass from the earth.

2 Samuel 23:3-4

We have good reasons to be concerned for those who govern and those who serve them. Although we have no kings in our country, leaders in positions of power can bring great blessing, like light after the night or lush green vegetation after rain. They can serve their constituents well and thus further a vibrant and growing community. They can help improve the economy and bring employment to a city or improve the health of families. They have the responsibility to be concerned with acts of mercy, and can make a difference to those in need. Solomon reminds them,

Speak up for those who cannot speak for themselves,
for the rights of all who are destitute.
Speak up and judge fairly;
defend the rights of the poor and needy.

Proverbs 31:8-9

This responsibility of government is often ignored, but Matthew 25 and other passages remind us that, individually and corporately, Christians have an obligation to demonstrate justice and mercy at home and abroad. Both the Old and New Testaments call God's people to care for the orphan and widow, those treated unjustly, and those in poverty or in prison. We may disagree about various government policies, but rather than arguing the pros and cons of laws that have been instituted, why not prayerfully influence those in government who administer such funds and activity? These civil servants spend much of their lives in this arena and can make a significant difference for millions who struggle. How can the church minister most effectively to those responsible for serving the community? How can we pray for them and their families? How well do we know their personal and work needs?

In Psalm 138, King David voices his concern for other leaders in the wider world: "May all the Kings of the earth praise you, O Lord, when they hear the words of your mouth. May they sing of the ways of the Lord, for the glory of the Lord is great." (verses 4-5) This concern expressed three millennia ago is relevant for the church today. Should we also not desire to see those in a nation's leadership think and speak well of God and his ways? My hope is that this psalm and prayer given thousands of years ago would represent both the desire and an intentional ministry of the church today.

"I'll lend you a book to read; it will show you that the world and all living things are quite different from what you imagine, and all this talk about God is sheer nonsense..."

—Joseph Stalin

"In a world in which logic shifted and disintegrated, it is not surprising that modern times did not develop in ways the generation of 1920 would have considered 'logical.' What is important in history is not only the events that occur but the events that obstinately do not occur. The outstanding event of modern time was the failure of religious belief to disappear."

—Paul Johnson, *Modern Times*

CHAPTER 2

PRAY AND SERVE WHOMEVER GOD PUTS BEFORE YOU IN THE HALLS OF GOVERNMENT

REV. DR. RODNEY WOOD

"Just pray. Don't be intrusive. Don't try to position yourself. Never look at a person's station in life. And serve whomever I put before you." Those are the words I heard in my heart on a Saturday afternoon in January of 1993 as my wife Becky and I stood alone in the rotunda of the Louisiana State Capitol.

It has been my privilege to serve the men and women of the Louisiana Legislature and other governmental leaders of our state for over 20 years. I am very grateful for the invitation to share about my calling to this work and the manner in which I have sought to carry it out. I pray that as you read my story, as well as the thoughts of other contributors to this book, some of you will be called by God to go to your state capitols or city halls and engage in ministry to those in government. I also pray that *every one of you* will be moved to greater intentionality with regard to your ministry of prayer and encouragement to those in public office.

It will be helpful if I begin by telling you a bit about my background.

I come from a very long line of Louisianans. My family has been in Louisiana for more than 200 years. My great-great-great-grandfather fought with Colonel Andrew Jackson in the Battle of New Orleans. Another of my great-grandfathers died in office while serving in the House of Representatives when New Orleans was the capital in the mid-1800s. I could go on with more family history, but my point is this: I'm a Louisianan, and I love the people of my state. Although I never told anyone, as a university student I had a strong desire to serve in government. I would sometimes go to the Capitol to study, and I remember standing on its steps and saying, "One day I am going to be here." Well, I was correct, but it was by a different path and for a different purpose than I ever imagined.

I realize that many of you are not natives of Louisiana, but I am sure that, wherever your home may be, you have always known about Louisiana's "colorful" politics.

When I was a boy in the 1950s, everybody was either a "Long" or an "Anti-Long" (supporter or opponent of those associated with the Long family). Emotions ran high during election years, and the stumping was quite a show. One of the most colorful stars of the show was "Uncle Earl" – Governor Earl K. Long. Uncle Earl once said that voters "don't want good government, they want good entertainment." He also joked that one day the people of Louisiana would "elect good government and they won't like it." That's the environment in which many of us Louisianans grew up.

So how was I called by God to minister at the Louisiana Capitol?

On a January afternoon in 1993, two of my sons and I were traveling through Baton Rouge on a hunting trip. I was serving as a pastor in Covington, Louisiana, at the time, and was in a period of intense prayer about my next step in ministry. As we passed by the

Capitol, suddenly I sensed that God was speaking to my heart, calling me to Baton Rouge and to service in the Capitol.

I admit that such a sudden moment of calling is a bit uncommon. But in the days that immediately followed, God did some very extraordinary things to give me strong and direct assurance that He was indeed calling me to this work.

I had no entrée. I had no invitation of any kind. But I had the certainty of His calling.

So, on Saturday afternoon, January 23rd, my wife Becky and I drove to Baton Rouge and walked hand in hand up the Capitol steps and into the very empty and quiet rotunda. I remember standing there asking the Lord, "What if these people don't want my ministry here?" And immediately I heard, as if spoken to, "Don't worry about that. Just pray."

"Just pray?" I asked. "Just pray" echoed within me. Then these words of instruction came clearly to my mind:

- Don't be intrusive.
- Don't try to position yourself.
- Never look at a person's station in life.
- And serve whomever I put before you.

Becky and I then got on the elevator and went up 27 floors to the lookout tower of the Capitol. We walked out on the observation deck and prayed to the Lord, committing ourselves to do His bidding.

That summer we established The Mission Foundation and moved to Baton Rouge to start our work. I began to lead a men's ministry in the city, and every Thursday afternoon the year around for the next six and a half years, I prayed at the Capitol – in the House chamber, in the Senate chamber, and then up at the top where I could walk around the tower and pray, looking toward the north, the south, the east, and the west.

In the spring months, when the legislature was in session, I went to the Capitol more often, and sat in the gallery and prayed for the legislators and simply remained available to anyone. As the years passed, as I had an ever-present, private longing for a fuller ministry, I prayed, "If You want me to do this ('just pray') for the rest of my life, You're going to have to help me. Please help me."

During those years, God blessed me with many wonderful friendships – friendships with the guards, the receptionists, and other workers in the building. Also, little by little, God worked in various ways to bless me with true friendships with senators and representatives and other governmental leaders. However, it was not until May of 1996 that I was first asked to open the House of Representatives in prayer, and two years later that I was invited for my first time to lead the Senate in prayer.

Then finally, in January of 2000, members of the legislature asked me to do that for which I had long hoped but had never mentioned. For several years, they had held a weekly, private, early morning prayer meeting, which was an informal time of sharing and praying among a handful of very devoted legislators. To my great delight, after six and a half years, they asked me if I would come and lead them! This marked the beginning of the Louisiana Legislators' Bible Study/Prayer Breakfast, which will soon begin its 15th year.

Well, that's how it happened. But who comes? And what do we do?

The Legislators' Bible Study/Prayer Breakfast is for senators and representatives only. There are no guests. We meet in a private chamber in the basement of the Capitol where they can freely express themselves. No constituents are looking at them or listening to them. It's a safe place – away from evaluating eyes and ears. It's a place where they can open their hearts to one another.

This fellowship of men and women is a very diverse group – politically, racially, and denominationally. There are Democrats and Republicans, Catholics and Protestants, and a great variety of political and theological perspectives. Yet they enjoy the very warmest friendship! The brotherly and sisterly affection among them is truly remarkable. Since the days when they and I first began meeting, political differences have been left at the door. We have fixed our hearts and minds on our common love for the Savior and on our love for one another and for the people of our state.

We focus on only two things: the study of God's Word and prayer. I prepare and distribute a weekly handout, and the legislators open the Holy Scriptures and read and study and seek to apply the Scriptures to their lives. They also share prayer requests and pray for the needs of individuals around the state and for God's guidance and strength for themselves.

In 2013, I launched a new initiative in our ministry: The Louisiana Legislators' Regional Prayer Luncheons. During the weeks prior to the session, I traveled to various parts of the state to lead these prayer luncheons. We studied the leadership qualities of Nehemiah, who was governor of Jerusalem, and the representatives and senators prayed that God would give them those qualities. Then, one after another, they offered petitions to God regarding the needs of their regions, as they prayed . . .

- for those in poverty, for the elderly, the unemployed and under-employed.
- for our schools and institutions of higher education, including vo-tech schools.
- for our industry, agriculture, medical care, emergency response, prisons, environmental concerns, and for churches and pastors.
- for themselves – for wisdom, for spiritual vitality and protection against temptation, for mental and physical strength, and for unity in spite of their differences. And they prayed for their families.

Every year, at the beginning of the session, we turn to verses 1-7 of Romans 13 for our legislators to experiencing a renewed awareness of their calling as God's appointed ministers of justice. The Apostle Paul's words remind them that they are in their offices ultimately because God has sovereignly placed them there. Through this passage, they are also called to remember that they are "God's servants," His "agents of justice" for the people. We then turn to Proverbs 31 to listen again to the strong instruction that a young king named Lemuel received from his mother. She says to her son, "Speak up for those who cannot speak for themselves, for the rights of all who are destitute. Speak up and judge fairly; defend the rights of the poor and needy." Twice she says, "Speak up!" That is, give voice to those who have no voice! The temptation of the governmental leader is to give voice to those who *do* have a voice – to be particularly attentive to those who have influence, who have clout.

Also, during the months that the legislature is in session, I continue to spend time in each chamber praying and being available to anyone, as I did during the early years. Unless I am ministering out of the country, I very often pray on Thursday afternoons when they are not in session.

So what change have we seen?

I am very happy to tell you that in the mid-'90s, winds of significant change began to blow. I am aware, of course, of the scandals and criminal convictions of some of our statewide elected officials, including those who have served in Washington. But such things have not been characteristic of our state legislature during the past couple of decades. God has brought about a marvelous change!

I want to be careful to point out that good men and women served in our legislature before that time, and I appreciate all that they did. However, in the past twenty years, a steadily increasing number of sincere, godly men and women have been called by God to serve in our House of Representatives and Senate.

Also, some of those who were already in office have become more forthright, more open about their faith. During this past session, a senator who has served in the legislature for many years and is a highly respected leader, said to me, "Things aren't the way they used to be around here. They've changed. And listen, I've changed!"

I give thanks to our Lord for that testimony. And even if tomorrow morning we were to hear on the news about the worst scandal in the last 50 years, I would tell you with no less confidence that in both the House of Representatives and the Senate there are many men and women of the highest integrity, including those who have been in office for a very long time. They, of course, need our prayers. They are subjected to great pressures and temptations every day.

How has this change come about?

The change that has taken place over the past couple of decades has been the result of the prayers and other ministry involvements of many pastors and lay people in Louisiana. Most of this work has been quietly carried out in ways that are not widely known.

However, some people have engaged in well-organized and more highly visible efforts. One organization has sought to influence public policy through lobbying. Another organization was formed for intercessory ministry, and they have faithfully prayed at the Capitol for many years. Also, as in other states, Louisiana has a committee of lay people who work very hard on the annual Governor's Prayer Breakfast, where men and women throughout the state come together to be led by elected officials in Scripture reading and intercessory prayer and to hear a gospel-centered message from a guest speaker.

My own work has been described by others as a "chaplaincy" to the House and Senate, although I was never officially appointed to such a position. Years ago, a freshman member of the House of Representatives who was not involved in the weekly Bible Study/ Prayer Breakfast, spoke to me about his desire to have an appointed chaplain (which, by the way, was later done). I told him that I felt that it was best to carry on as we had been doing – that is, that the ministry to the legislators would be done simply on a relational basis. I was concerned that the role might at some point become politicized. I am not saying that a formal appointment cannot be a positive step. In fact, there are ministers who serve in this way quite effectively. However, I do believe that we must be on our guard at all times to protect the integrity of a chaplaincy kind of ministry.

I have often reflected on the words of Jesus in John 15:14-15: "You are my friends . . . . I have called you friends . . . ." These words are foundational to authentic ministry. However, friendship can be feigned, and often is. A minister can even deceive himself into thinking that he is being a real friend when in fact he is more self-focused than he realizes. So, on many early mornings, as I have walked across the Capitol grounds on my way to the Louisiana Legislators' Bible Study/Prayer Breakfast, I have asked our heavenly Father to fill my heart with genuineness. We must be *true* friends to those whose hands we shake in places of power.

I am now 63 years old. If God would so allow it, I would like very much to serve "whomever (He) puts before me" at the Louisiana State Capitol for another 20 years!

CHAPTER 3

PRAYER FOR THOSE IN AUTHORITY

GLENN PARKINSON

In 1968, I represented Annapolis High School in its annual Youth Constitutional Convention, an opportunity for future leaders to draft their own constitution from the Senate Chamber in the city's historic State House. My largest contribution was an unpopular rant to remove any reference to God in the document. I had been a convinced atheist for years, and was unashamed in my arguments against religious superstition and bigotry.

One year later, the Lord very graciously revealed to me that I was an idiot, an idiot that he loved very much. I discovered the Lord Jesus, and rediscovered all of life through him. Under good teaching, I confessed and made restitution for every past sin which the Holy Spirit brought to mind. The list included a few sins from several categories, and some were difficult, like confessing petty shoplifting and paying for what I had taken years after the fact. The one sin I could not think how to make restitution for was what I had said on the floor of the Senate.

Forty-three years later, in 2011, and as a seasoned minister in the Presbyterian Church in America, I attended an open hearing conducted by the Maryland General Assembly as part of its consideration of the Civil Marriage Protection Act (authorizing gay marriage). I went principally to argue that the issue should be put to referendum – as it eventually was.

I arrived for the hearing early, and filled the time by leisurely walking through the old State House. When I walked into the Senate Chambers, I was shocked to find myself weeping. The memory of my blasphemous high school opposition to God filled me with grief. I knew I was forgiven, of course, but I grieved over an inability to make things right in terms of my witness and his glory.

Two weeks later, I received an invitation to lead the Maryland Senate in prayer! What a gracious Father we have. He saw the grief in my heart, and for my own joy, as well as his glory, arranged for me to stand in that very room and pray in the name of his Son.

That is how God got my attention. A year later, I was again asked to lead in prayer. This time, however, I was asked to submit my prayer ahead of time. I was subsequently contacted by phone and asked to remove the words, "in Jesus' name." I was informed that it was against policy to speak of Jesus on the floor of the Senate – in prayer, at least. I declined, and have not been invited back since.

In this chapter I will make two contributions to the subject of prayer for civil authorities. The first is a sermon preached on the classic text of 1 Timothy 2:1-8. The second is a suggestion about how we might practically deal with this messy business of praying in the context of civil functions.

> I urge, then, first of all, that requests, prayers, intercession and thanksgiving be made for everyone—for kings and all those in authority, that we may live peaceful and quiet lives in all godliness and holiness. This is good, and pleases God our Savior, who wants all men to be saved and to come to a knowledge of the truth.

> For there is one God and one mediator between God and men, the man Christ Jesus, who gave himself as a ransom for all men—the testimony given in its proper time. And for this purpose I was appointed a herald and an apostle—I am telling the truth, I am not lying—and a teacher of the true faith to the Gentiles.
>
> I want men everywhere to lift up holy hands in prayer, without anger or disputing.
>
> 1 Timothy 2:1-8 (NIV)

The Big Picture

In this text, Paul sets prayer for government leaders in a larger context. Understanding this context is critical for understanding the purpose of such prayers. The request to pray for kings is sandwiched inside a larger topic. Paul's main focus was not our government leaders. He urged us to lift them up in prayer for a greater reason.

Paul's reference to kings is a spontaneous insertion of thought. Paul's main point was to pray for *everyone*. Praying specifically for kings somehow supports that larger idea. The focus of our prayers is for Christ's redemption to reach everyone in the community – that is, all segments of society. Not just the high born and powerful, but the low born and oppressed. Not just the slave owner, but the slave. Not just men, but women and children. We must focus first on that main idea if we are to appreciate why Paul spontaneously sandwiched in a reference to kings. The Book of Acts reveals that when Paul visited a new town, he ministered to the wealthy and the poor, to slaves and civil servants, to men, women and whole households—to everyone. Paul's concern was to reach every part of society with the gospel of Jesus Christ. This was central to his strategy to demonstrate that the gospel is a gift of grace and can never favor any class or strata of society.

To get the gist of Paul's overall intent, see how the text flows without the sandwiched comment about government:

> I urge, then, first of all, that requests, prayers, intercession and thanksgiving be made for everyone. This is good, and pleases God our Savior, who wants all men to be saved and to come to a knowledge of the truth.
>
> For there is one God and one mediator between God and men, the man Christ Jesus, who gave himself as a ransom for all men—the testimony given in its proper time. And for this purpose I was appointed a herald and an apostle ...

God wants all kinds of people saved. Of course, God knows the end from the beginning and has decreed from eternity past the individuals he will bring to himself. Paul was not thinking here of God's eternal decrees, but rather what the Bible tells us about God's plan in history. The Bible says that God has resolved to draw to himself people of every description, from every strata of society, eventually from every nation on earth. He will do this so that no sinner can ever boast before him—no ethnic or national group, no level of IQ, no gender or caste can claim special treatment. To show favor or disfavor to any human distinction would undermine a gospel of sovereign grace (1 Corinthians 1:26-29).

Therefore, you could not find in any society any group of people that God does not intend to raid with the gospel, rescuing at least some—perhaps many—from destruction. God wants the gospel of his Son proclaimed everywhere, and he will save anyone who embraces it. He is determined to save people from every nook and cranny on earth.

Sad to say, God's purposes are not always ours. In every culture, Christians of one stripe seem to have a very hard time believing that people of another stripe can equally be saved. And yet conservatives, liberals, the homeless, the wealthy one percent, the nondescript, the famous, the criminal, the hero – God will save some of each of them, and every kind of person in between. There is no sort of sinner that God is *not* interested in redeeming. He wants all kinds of sinners to repent, receive his forgiveness and become citizens in his eternal kingdom.

The Lord has decreed that the way he will reach them is through the gospel shared by us. So, what sort of prayers will he want to hear from his people? "I urge, then, first of all, that requests, prayers, intercession and thanksgiving be made for everyone .... This is good, and pleases God our Savior, who wants all men to be saved and to come to a knowledge of the truth." Prayer is a means established by God to empower his gospel and draw people to himself. When we pray, God involves us in accomplishing his will on earth as it is in heaven.

Often our prayers for the spread of the gospel are answered indirectly. None of us has personal access to everyone in our society. So God answers our prayers by raising up other Christians and working through them. But it all evens out, because other Christians are praying for people they can't reach, and God raises *us* up in answer to their prayers. Are you praying for someone to reach out to your grandson away at college? Well, somebody from another culture may be praying for someone to reach out to a family member who happens to work right next to you. As long as we have political and social freedom to share the gospel across lines of age, race, gender, and culture, every kind of person can be reached.

Prayer for Authorities

As Paul dictated this exhortation to pray the gospel into every corner of society, he interjected a thought which may well have been stimulated by where this letter was going: Ephesus. Earlier in this letter, Paul urged Timothy to "stay there in Ephesus" (1 Timothy 1:3). Ephesus was a center of Paul's work, and crucial to the spread of the gospel in Asia Minor.

Ephesus had been the scene of a massive riot instigated by the silversmith guild (Acts 19:23-41). The guild was angry because increasing numbers of Christians had lost interest in silver idols of Artemis, patron goddess of the city, thus crippling their business. The silversmiths tried to give the new Christian church a bad name in Ephesus by labeling them irreligious (they didn't worship the local goddess), unpatriotic and uncivil (they didn't support the Temple of Artemis, the backbone of city's culture). Apparently, Paul had intentionally cultivated a friendship with the town fathers who were, presumably, open to this new gospel. But they were terrified at the prospect of possible Roman repercussions to riots in their streets. If this new religion were going to be a source of civil unrest and disharmony, if Christians were a bunch of troublemakers, then the town would want no part of them.

So, as Paul instructed Timothy to pray to reach all segments of society, he interjected an instruction about kings. I'm sure if he had had a word processor, the effect would be more elegant, but what he wrote is perfectly clear: "I urge, then, first of all, that requests, prayers, intercession and thanksgiving be made for everyone (for kings and all those in authority, that we may live peaceful and quiet lives in all godliness and holiness). This is good and pleases God our Savior, who wants all men to be saved."

Notice that the goal of these prayers for civil authorities is clearly stated. It is not to lobby God for particular legislation. However fine such prayers may be, Paul here instructs us to pray for those in authority *so that* we may live out our faith peacefully and quietly.

Why is that so important? Because God wants to use his church to reach *everyone* with the gospel of his Son. He answers our prayers to accomplish this, and that's why we are instructed to pray for civil authorities. Paul's assumption is that the propagation of the gospel to all segments of a culture is most robust when the church and its society are at peace.

War, disease, and poverty tend to separate people into competing camps. Keeping the community secure, healthy and reasonably prosperous is the king's job. We pray for the king to do his job well, so that barriers between people will be lower, and the gospel can reach everyone.

If our authorities won't do their job minimally well, God will give the nation to someone else who will. Such transitions are often nightmarish, when a healthy version of the gospel is hard to find amidst the dense undergrowth of superstition and fear. In the darkness of social upheaval, factions become even more protective and hostile, making it yet harder for Christians to reach out across classes and races.

That is why we pray for those in authority, whoever they are. We can pray about all kinds of things regarding our culture. But first we pray that our authorities will govern a society in which the church can live in peace. The lower the barriers separating the church from other subgroups, the better Christians can make friends across those barriers, bringing the gospel with them.

It is true that by God's grace, the church can prosper without peace, even under persecution. Toward the beginning of the third century, the Christian leader Tertullian responded to Roman abuse, "Your tortures accomplish nothing, though each is more refined than the last; rather they are an enticement to our religion. We become more every time we are hewn down by you: the blood of Christians is seed [for the church]." Wherever faith is held fast under pressure, even unto death, others will grow to admire it. Communism could not stamp out the gospel in Russia. China can't do it today.

The fact that the gospel can prosper in persecution, however, does not make that the best situation for the gospel, or we would be told to pray for martyrdom. Instead, the apostles encourage us to live at peace with all men and strive for a good reputation in our community so that we are welcome to pursue our faith.

Such peaceful freedom is the goal of our prayer for those in authority: "that we may live peaceful and quiet lives in all godliness and holiness." Peaceful, or tranquil, living suggests freedom from external pressures and conflict. A quiet life tends to be free from internal anxiety and fear. We need peaceable relations with our society so we can exercise the godliness and holiness that will help us reach *everyone* in our culture with the gospel. The gospel does not reach every subgroup in a culture all at once. It reaches one group. From there, it must reach out to all the other groups. For the spread of the gospel, this is most important.

So, this is what Paul tells us to pray for. Nothing about the exposure of infants or the horrors of gladiatorial games – not even anything about Nero's excesses and looming threat. Of course Christians will pray about such things quite naturally. But Paul instructed us "first of all" to pray for our civic leaders to rule in such a way that we could live peaceful and quiet lives, allowing our godliness and holiness to shine. This is because God our Savior "wants all men to be saved and to come to a knowledge of the truth."

Of course, this priority exists in tension with our practice of justice and mercy. History has shown how seductive state power can be to the church. Christ's church must not sacrifice its identity or message currying state favor or turning a blind eye to oppression.

Even so, Paul urged us to pray, as of first importance, for evangelism and church planting that brings the gospel to every segment of society. The best way every segment of society can be reached is with a church that is allowed to pursue its goals peacefully and without restriction, and that depends largely on the governing authorities doing their job well.

Of course, the church can grow amidst persecution, and sometimes persecution can have a spiritually cleansing effect. But the gospel is less effective when local leaders lead the general populace to hate it or scorn it. The church is not penetrating Arab society and European society today because it is persecuted in the one, and scorned in the other.

In contrast, the period of greatest gospel outreach in modern times was when Great Britain and the United States, as cultures, became friends of the church. I'm not trying to defend English colonialism or American foreign policy; being friends with the church does not make a society and its government holy. But it does, as a by-product, encourage evangelism. Missionaries sent out from England and America reached more people in the last 150 years than at any time since the days of the New Testament. That was the result of the church being able to peacefully pursue its mission.

Praise God for hardy church remnants that remain rooted through the avalanche and grow in the darkness of the catacombs. But praise God even more for the church that blossoms over miles and miles of acreage, prospering and transforming an entire countryside. In God's providence, the church can use the friendship and respect of its society, and of civil authorities in particular, to take the gospel to *everyone* in the land. So we pray for civil authorities that we may lead a peaceful and quiet life, free to explore our faith, live it out, and offer it to every subculture around us.

Building Bridges Instead of Walls

Paul was never one to hide the truth or mince words, especially where the gospel was concerned. But he was painfully aware that the truth of the gospel can be obscured when Christians are thought of as civil troublemakers. As Paul traveled around the Mediterranean speaking to Gentiles, he treated the societies he visited with respect, and the Gentiles respectfully listened as he proclaimed Christ. He was welcome in the marketplace and wherever people exchanged ideas.

Then Paul came to Ephesus, the city he hoped would become the hub of the church in that region. He must have looked forward to the annual festival, when thousands would come to worship the idol

Artemis. What an opportunity to proclaim Christ! But those thousands of people never heard the gospel during that festival. They were stirred up by special interest groups who unfairly called Christians names and labeled them as bad influences—as people intent on taking their society apart. They got away with it because Christians had not had the time to build a reputation there. So instead of hearing the good news of Jesus Christ, the citizens shouted, "Great is Artemis of the Ephesians," for two hours. It was impossible for Paul to even speak to the crowd. That day, they were mindlessly opposed to this Christianity, whatever it was.

Paul had prayed for the citizens and visitors in Ephesus, because God wants all men to be saved and come to a knowledge of the truth. He had especially prayed for the Ephesian civic leaders, whose friendship he had intentionally cultivated. But as thousands left the city prejudiced against the gospel that could have saved them, Paul realized that his prayers would have to be answered another day, when the prayers of an established Ephesian church would join his own before God's throne.

It is usually bad for the gospel when civil authorities see Christians as part of the problems they must deal with instead of part of the solution. Sometimes that antipathy is brought on by zealous Christians who treat anyone within government who does not share a biblical world view as an enemy. Unfortunately, such nastiness abounds among conservative Christians, and saturates social media. How can we partner with and befriend people we mock and despise? How can we expect them to treat us any differently?

Sometimes the antipathy is brought on by zealous secularists who are allergic to anything religious. I experienced that myself when my invitation to open the Maryland Senate in prayer was withdrawn because my submitted prayer contained the name, "Jesus Christ." Who lost in that decision? The State of Maryland is the poorer for filtering out exposure to religious thinking. The Church loses, too, as we are increasingly marginalized.

But the larger point is that *all the people of Maryland* lose when the gospel is filtered out of public discourse. Many subgroups in Maryland remain far from the gospel, and reaching them is helped along when our government and society at large have a place for us at their table. Conversely, when church and state are needlessly at odds with each other, it is harder to invite all groups of people to Christ's table. Hostility encourages wall-building; it thrives on self-protection and demonizing opposition. Hostility encourages a shell around the church – from the outside perspective, isolating us, and from the inside perspective, protecting us. It is just harder to reach out from a shell.

Christians are called to bring the gospel to every people group in their society. For us, that means every race and minority, every political persuasion, people with every degree of education or wealth, healthy people, disabled people, young and old, homemakers and career women, singles and people who are single again, married couples and single parents, heterosexuals, homosexuals, criminals, prison inmates, soccer moms, illegal aliens, CEO's, drug dealers, men and women in the military, adult children still living at home, movie makers, porn queens, tenured professors, politicians, celebrities, plumbers, cartoonists, engineers, lobbyists … *everyone*.

God wants all kinds of sinners to be saved. That is why he is so pleased when he hears his people praying for *everyone*. It is why he is especially pleased when we pray for his blessing upon our civil authorities to the end that we avoid a hostile, antagonistic reputation that would harden our society against us and hinder us from reaching all kinds of people with the gospel.

Praying for civil authorities does not guarantee that we will escape persecution. In just a few years, Paul and the churches he wrote to would be persecuted. In fact, everyone who wants to live a godly life in Christ Jesus will be persecuted (2 Timothy 3:12). But let's not cultivate animosity. People may reject the gospel for fear of God's rule, but they should not reject it for fear of us. When angry Christians threaten and posture and pontificate, when a society hears only militant determination to impose our views and our rules, they defensively keep us out instead of letting Christ in. Things don't have to be that way.

A member of my congregation who is administrative assistant to a state delegate kindly obtained an appointment for me with the delegate. The first fifteen minutes or so were cordially polite, as this civil servant waited for another pastor to vent his political views. Eventually, however, he realized that I was not there to grill him or tell him how to do his job. I was there to learn how to pray for him. I kept my ears open and learned a thing or two about him and his family. Then, I asked him my principal question: "What do you think is the greatest problem facing our community?" I wanted to know what he had to deal with. I heard not only about a particular issue, but also about some of the immense roadblocks that made progress so difficult. I learned something of how to pray for him, that he might do his job well.

I repeated the experience with a state senator from the other side of the aisle. Again the polite dance until he understood that I came to listen, not preach. This was his office, not my pulpit, and I was visiting him. Again I asked what he thought the biggest problem was in our community. Again I learned something.

I then met with a judge. He was eager to talk about the problems he saw. What I came away with surprised me. All three of those men pointed out the same problem as the worst one they faced every day: the breakdown of the family. Before I left, they each told me that if the church could do anything to help in that area, they would be grateful. I got the distinct impression that if we did, they would consider us an ally. That plea should influence the strategy of our congregation. It is, in effect, an invitation to pursue our faith outside of our congregation and into the community.

What about praying in the Senate Chamber? I spoke to my state senator about the name of Jesus being excluded from prayer in the state senate. I even suggested another way forward. My senator was more than sympathetic, but said that political realities were not on my side right now. The time will come, I hope, when I can try again.

What is the suggestion I'll come back with? Instead of asking clergy to *lead* the Senate in prayer, why not invite religious representatives to come and pray *for* the Senate? Leading in prayer assumes that everyone is being asked to pray, and that everyone is allowing you to speak to God for them. Personally, I agree that this notion is ludicrous and offensive in a pluralistic society. I would not want a leader of another faith to speak to God for me, using assumptions I would find untrue and even blasphemous. Of all people, evangelical Christians should understand this. We cannot speak to God *on behalf* of people who do not know him and perhaps do not care to. We can pray for them, but not as their spokesman.

Instead, we should replace *leading* public gatherings in prayer with praying *for* a public gathering. As part of a group being prayed for, I have no objection to someone of a different faith exercising their right to pray by praying for me. There is no potentially offensive assumption that this person represents me before God. I can reject their god, yet still respect their freedom and appreciate their good will.

If we substituted praying *for* instead of *leading* in prayer, prayer at public assemblies could become a religiously robust expression of a society's spiritual variety, instead of the colorless, tasteless or even silent thing I see it becoming. In proportion to their numbers in Maryland, I say let Muslims pray for the Senate; let atheists come to wish them well. And in proportion to our numbers, let Christian ministers pray freely for the Senate, glorifying God and seeking his blessing on our state along with the redemption of many, in the name of Jesus.

I hope to generate some discussion of this approach.

What could your church do, to minister the gospel while serving as an ally to those in authority?

Let's pray for those in authority, that we might have the freedom to pursue our faith openly. This will please God our Savior, who wants people of all kinds to be saved and to come to a knowledge of the truth.

"For, if we consider how heavy the burden of government is, and how much the welfare of any people depends on the zeal and godly conversation of those that have the rule over them: if we set before us the many dangers and difficulties, to which governors by their station are exposed, and the continual temptations they be under to luxury and self-indulgence; we shall not only pity, but pray for them…"

—George Whitefield, 18th Century

CHAPTER 4

OKLAHOMA

BOBBY GRIFFITH

I was the *last* person you wanted at the Oklahoma State Capitol. I remember thinking those words when Chuck Garriott asked me to consider taking over the Ministry to State study. In fact, I told him so. You *don't* want a pastor like me. I'm young. I'm apolitical. I don't wear suits every day. In fact, I barely wear them on Sunday. Sometimes I don't shave! You have to have "the look" to spend time at the Capitol. You have to be persuasive, enjoy spending time with politicians and not be a cynic!

But there was more. I keenly remember my earliest times at Heritage Presbyterian Church from 2001 until moving to St. Louis for seminary in 2003. The Capitol Bible Study was an important ministry. Governors and congressmen spoke there, and elected officials attended. This was a key ministry. This was something you didn't want to ruin.

Fast forward to 2009. I was a church planting resident in Norman, OK. Chuck was in Washington, D.C., flying to Oklahoma City nearly once a month to speak. This key ministry was not as robust as it once had been because there was no local leader to take ownership.

From 2009 until 2011, I occasionally filled in to speak. Imagine my fear the first time I walked into the Governor's Large Conference Room ten minutes before the event began. Lunch was catered, and people began to file in with plates of food. I noticed something – these were normal people like me. They were hungry, not just for food, but for prayer and to hear the gospel. During these two years, I made the drive from Norman to the Capitol a few times. I cannot say I fell in love with this hour and a half of my life, but I did see the value. I was buying in, but happy to stay on the margins. Then Chuck approached me with a proposition that would change things.

During 2011, Chuck and I had numerous conversations on the phone, in person and through email. "Will you take over this ministry?" He had to ask more than once, of course, but by that fall, I committed. The Capitol Bible study was now in my hands and was a ministry of our church plant in downtown Oklahoma City.

For the first year, I floundered and nearly killed this Bible study that had been in place since the 1990s! How?

In retrospect, I didn't *love* this ministry. I stepped in because there was a need and I was in the best position to fill it. It was logical. But there was more than that. I failed to do the most important thing in ministry: pay attention to Christ's example in John 1:14 (ESV) "and the Word became flesh and dwelled among us…." I was present, but not incarnate.

Let me tell you how I almost killed a ministry.

Chuck flew to Oklahoma City every four to six weeks to speak. Pete, another local pastor, spoke the second Wednesday each month. Ministry to State provided lunch, and two volunteers committed to serve it every week. With this built-in support, as a ministry leader I *knew* I had a base on which to build and grow the group that averaged around 20 a week. Chuck provided mentoring. Pete was the dynamic second-week speaker. I had enough pastor friends and ministry contacts to bring in interesting speakers. This is the perfect situation for someone who did not have to start from scratch.

Instead, 2012 was a year of decline. I was there nearly every Wednesday, but not really present. In retrospect, I do not believe I really believed in this ministry. I still held on to my apathy toward the symbolism the Capitol represented even though most of the attendees were not elected officials. I liked the group a lot—it was racially, socially and denominationally diverse. But I had a problem connecting, and there was no cohesiveness. And, to be honest, my heart was not in it. I showed up at 11:50, ate, talked with a few folks, took prayer requests quickly, moved to the lesson, ended and went on my way. Granted, life was busy because we were planting a growing church, I was finishing my Ph.D. coursework, and trying to have some semblance of a home life.

Still, John 1:14 had not taken hold. Add to that some retirements and budget cuts during 2012, and I saw this group of 20 dwindle to down to six or seven on some weeks. By the fall of 2012, I questioned if I could continue and if we needed to shut this ministry down.

Then something happened. One regular attendee had a very traumatic life event – divorce. His wife told him she wanted out even though he wanted to reconcile. He bravely shared this during our prayer request time. He was honest. He was raw. Something clicked within me—John 1:14. If this ministry was to continue, I needed to make changes that reflected a commitment to loving the Capitol, and demonstrate the vulnerability that I show the congregation I serve.

What did I do? (2013 reboot)

We needed some serious changes. In December, I rebranded Capitol Bible Study to Capitol Forum and created handout cards for folks to invite their co-workers. Still, I realized this ministry would not grow or flourish if I were the main event.

First, I needed a good plan that set the tone for the year. I had treated this ministry as something I could parachute down into and then leave. I did this even though I knew people do not respond well to that type of ministry. Part of it was my struggle with the call to do all this: church planting. Ph.D. program. Life. Family. Second, this one hour during the week needed to be something people looked forward to attending. I needed to reevaluate every aspect of this event and see what worked. I needed to take what did not work and get rid of it. Some of that was simple. For instance, we had relied on a vendor for several years to deliver one lunch a month. Over time, the quality greatly diminished. Quick fix – a new vendor.

I had to ask the question that noted speaker and marketer Simon Sinek says every good leader considers: *Why? Why is this ministry needed?* As I consulted with a leadership development coach in late 2012, he suggested I answer this question.

I realized that this ministry needed to exist because *it provides a place of rest and support for the Capitol community*. You see, the biblical answer to all our problems is shalom, wholeness, and flourishing. That one hour a week needs to be a place where people are invited to come in their weariness and enter into rest.

How did we do that?

In my short life I have learned that you can build community when you provide a solid purpose for it to exist. An acquaintance of mine operates an inner city ministry that reaches kids who have little guidance in their lives. These kids have nothing; they walk the line between the juvenile justice system and state custody. My friend and his father invest in them so they do not become gang members, drug dealers, pimps and prostitutes. Every December, they have a clothing drive so poor kids can have a coat, some warm clothes and, honestly, feel dignified. The week before this event, I asked the folks at Capitol Forum to bring something for the kids. I would gather the items the next week and deliver them. Imagine my surprise when people overwhelmingly responded with generosity!

This also helped me to make a big change in Capitol Forum. As I planned the 2013 calendar, I realized this community needed to be challenged. I told the group I was going to regularly bring in leaders from the local Christian nonprofit community to challenge us with an emphasis on the *love your neighbor* aspect of the gospel. Jesus calls us to enter into brokenness, and the Oklahoma City metro area is a place that is at the bottom of so many statistics – from divorce to child welfare to teen pregnancies to foster care – and we demonstrate the gospel by loving others.

We sprang into 2013 with new and interesting speakers. John Sowers, author of *Fatherless Generation*, spoke about the Bible's storyline: *God wants to be with us*. He challenged our folks to respond to the needs in our city. There is a large homeless colony just two blocks from the Capitol, and my friend Rev. Treb Praytor talked about how churches and individuals can reach these "outcasts" for Christ. Treb shared how his church ministers to that population, and how they are also working to provide transitional housing for single mothers. Valerie Sherrer with Novo Ministries shared how churches can partner with her ministry of reconciliation to reach inner city kids with the gospel. One person responded and sent Novo's information to their church to partner with them!

In the first few months of 2013, the emphasis of Capitol Forum began to change from information to transformation. We kept asking, how can we be people who respond to God's call to love him and love others?

Another way we asked that question was in our prayer time. I hate confessing this, but our prayer time had become fairly stale after I took over. But this changed. When one of our attendees opened up about his process of divorce, this became a weekly prayer with updates. We built the relational space for me to ask a follow up question when he opened up about the divorce, his kids and his soon-to-be ex-wife. This seemed to lift a veil, and people *felt* and *saw* they had the freedom to be open about life.

Soon, others began to share serious things in their lives. One woman shared her struggles with watching her husband become more and more ill. She was open with her anger, pain, and sadness. We also journeyed with a man who had an alcohol-addicted son. We prayed for the son's recovery. He went to rehab, got a job and fell off the wagon. We prayed again for his recovery.

There is something powerful about creating space for people to be vulnerable and honest, knowing they can rely on others to pray and care for them. The prayer time went from a "request and prayer" that lasted five minutes to FIFTEEN! That is good and scary at the same time. It is good because people want to be cared for and listened to, especially when they have great needs. It is scary because people began to share heavy things.

I became more open with the folks who attended every week. I had grown up with the model that pastors do not struggle. They are super Christians who have strong faith, rarely sin and do not open up to others. Why should they? They are supposed to be an example! But when I read the Gospels, I see Jesus as someone who was tempted, but did not sin. Jesus lived in deep community with others. He wept when his friend, Lazarus, died. He sweat drops of blood because of the stress and pain of the cross before him. Paul tells us that Jesus emptied himself and became nothing.

So I opened up about my own struggles during prayer time. My wife and I both have infertility issues, and I finally had the guts to talk about it. We were on a long road to adopt a little boy from Kansas City, and the process had not gone well for a long time. I talked about my own fears and doubts and dropped the super-pastor pretense. People prayed for me. I actually felt human. I believe I appeared human.

A few months ago, I forgot to pray for a specific request two weeks in a row. It was completely unintentional, as I try to group similar requests (sickness, jobs, and praise reports) together. We end around 12:55, so imagine my surprise when my phone rang at 1:10 with one of my regular attendees on the other end. He graciously engaged me and said one of the things he loved about the Capitol Forum is that there is an air of openness, and in that spirit he wondered why I forgot his request two weeks in a row. What could have resulted in his last time of attendance worked into a conversation of repentance, forgiveness and grace. I realized that we had truly become a place of rest and support for the Capitol community.

What Happened?

In 2012 I asked the question: does this ministry need to continue? At the end of 2013, I am glad it does. Despite layoffs and retirements, we have seen substantial numerical growth. This ministry, which had dwindled down to six people, averages over twenty weekly. We have had weeks with nearly forty people in attendance. Because of the odd scheduling in each government agency, it is difficult to have the same twenty folks attend every week. A core group attends nearly every week, and thirty-five to forty attend as their schedules allow.

I like to tell people that this is my favorite group to give Bible lessons or sermonettes to. Why? We have fundamentalists, Evangelicals, Roman Catholics and mainline Protestants. We have janitors, security guards, tax collectors, bureaucrats, politicians, legislative aides, interns and everyone in between. There are Democrats and Republicans. We are racially diverse, too. I may be one of the only Presbyterian pastors who has a ministry with only one other Presbyterian in attendance!

But, more importantly, this group has grown in community and life change. We celebrate together. We mourn death together. People invite their co-workers and even friends who work nearby.

Ministering to the Capitol community has been one of the hardest and easiest things I've done. The easy part is logistics if the right team is in place. With two volunteers who help with food and an administrative person who makes the arrangements, my main responsibility is showing up on time or making sure the right speaker is in place. The hard part is being *present*. People know when you are really invested in their lives. It shows. You know the legislative schedule. You know the important issues debated. You remember where people work and can ask intelligent questions about the stress they face during key times in the government. To be an example of incarnation in a state capitol, you have to know the rhythm and flow of their world.

Even though I am still cynical about politics, I have come to realize that those in government need Jesus to show up with this agenda – to love and serve the capitol community.

CHAPTER 5

GOD, GIVE ME THE HUMILITY OF JESUS

STEVE BOSTROM

I am naturally proud – and so are you. And what can we say about the arrogance of our leaders? What if our leaders were known for their humility?

When I was asked to contribute to this volume devoted to those who lead us as civil servants, many topics came to mind, but humility was the chief. When I sent the article in, I was asked to include more of the context of my ministry as well as my background and ministry history.

Who am I? I am approaching my 63rd birthday. I've pastored for 36 years. Decades ago, I interviewed a seminary grad for a position on the staff where I served as senior pastor. The candidate, his wife and I were seated in a restaurant. After ordering our meals, my first question was: "Who are you?" He did not miss a beat. "I am a sinner saved by grace, called to proclaim the matchless gospel of Jesus Christ." So am I.

Who am I? I am a great grandson of Lars Bostrom, a homesteading Swede who immigrated to Colorado in the late 1800s. I was raised in the plains and Rockies of Colorado. As a child attending a Vacation Bible School at the Bible Presbyterian Church of Colorado Springs (1958), I first heard and believed the gospel.

My parents were educators, and my three siblings and I thrived in school. With the launch of Sputnik in 1957, it appeared that the Russians were winning the space race. In 1960, a group of fourth graders in our city were given IQ tests. Those who scored well were gathered into two classes of HAT – Highly Academically Talented – students, and I was among them. I've had the privilege of having many great classmates and great teachers, but my best teacher is the Holy Spirit, who takes the Scriptures to 'hyper-remind' (Jn. 14:26) me of Jesus.

I graduated *magna cum laude* from both Westmont College and Covenant Seminary. I met my incomparable wife in 1974, and we married in 1976. God sent us one daughter and seven sons. We have eight grandchildren. I've pastored four churches, starting two of those, and closing the last one. I've held leadership positions in my denomination as well as in my community, and had the privilege of founding and chairing the board of a healthy adoption agency. I'm even the chaplain for our minor league baseball team. Currently, I serve as a pastor at large to the city of Helena, Montana.

Pride is, was, and will continue to be a constant temptation until I am taken to glory. Without effort or with great effort I can/could/will be a proud husband, proud father, proud Presbyterian, proud pastor, proud Montanan.

But God's kingdom is coming. All along the way, there has been a still, small voice: "Get low; God's grace flows downhill." And the voice of John the Baptist trumpets across the millennia: "He, Jesus, must increase and I must decrease."

As I've gotten older, God has given me more capacity to relate to the high and to the low. And so, the Greek word, "parakaleo," Jesus' favorite word for his Partner, the Holy Spirit, the "Paraclete," has become more of a reality. "Para" is: "alongside;" and "kaleo" is "to call."

"Parakaleo" sets the context for developing relationships with leaders, "coming alongside" civil servants to serve them as we can. Angels were sent to "deacon" ("minister to") Jesus when he was in need (Mt. 4:11). Ministry to State and organizations like it are not lobbyists; they seek to "minister." They serve and equip civil servants to fulfill the calling God has for them. It may be through a Bible study, a book, a quick coffee or lunch, or a heart-to-heart talk. Certainly, ministry includes prayer *for* them – and sometimes *with* them.

Ministry to such leaders is one of God's priorities. God told Ananias: "This man (Paul) is my chosen instrument to carry my name before the Gentiles *and their kings* and before the people of Israel" (Acts 9:15). God wants the "kings," those who serve in civil government, to know that a Person (One who is named, not an impersonal force) rules this universe. Those who know this Person are captivated by his humility. Let's pause and consider humility, particularly the humility described in the Bible and lived by Christ.

C S Lewis quotes the arresting words of his "father," George MacDonald: "The one principle of Hell is – 'I am my own!'" [9] And so Hell invades us and our world. We naturally live under the compulsion of dual mantras: "My life for me," and "Your life for me."

Henry Nouwen writes about the all-demanding self:

> What matters is how ***I*** am perceived by ***my*** world. If being busy is a good thing, then ***I*** must be busy. If having money is a sign of real freedom, then ***I*** must claim ***my*** money. If knowing many people proves ***my*** importance, ***I'll*** make

> the necessary contacts. The compulsion manifests itself in the lurking fear of failing and the steady urge to prevent this by gathering more of the same – more work, more money, more friends. [10]

But such pride will suffer violence when it hits the eternal wall of God's inscrutable will. It is humbling to learn that we have not achieved our places of honor by our own effort. Instead, God is the One who raises up those He chooses to place in positions of leadership. "I summon you by name and bestow on you a title of honor, though you do not acknowledge me" (Is 45:4). And, He may bring fools into positions of authority (Eccl 4:13). Ouch.

Our pride will also suffer violence when it hits the eternal wall of God's unchanging character. The message of God's life is: "My Life for yours." God, who humbled Himself to be born in Bethlehem and humbled Himself to be humiliated on the shameful cross, pursues those who will walk humbly with Him (Micah 5:8).

OK, is that enough to get your treadmill to slow down? Can you get off for a moment to ponder a paradigm shift?

Three different Bible authors did – authors separated by nearly one thousand years. The Holy Spirit motivated Solomon, James and Peter to tell us: "God opposes the proud but shows favor to the humble" (Proverbs 3:34; James 4:6; 1 Peter 5:5). When God speaks, we need to listen. When God repeats himself, we need to doubly prick up our ears. When God says something three times, we need to have Him write His words on our hearts.

When He writes on our hearts, we learn that above all else, we are to guard our hearts (Proverbs 4:23). Of course, we guard them from dangers; but, note that the father in Proverbs 23:6 asks his son to give him his heart. So, we also guard our hearts to give them away. In this case, we give them to the very personal truth of "God opposes the proud but shows favor to the humble."

"God *opposes* the proud." The Greek word that Peter and James use is a military term: *antitassó*. *Antí* means "opposite to, against," and *tássō* means "to arrange, to put in order." In other words, this is *organized resistance*, like an army assuming a specific battle-array position, bringing all its resources to resist its opponent.

Imagine the omnipotent God of the universe marshaling all his power and his angelic forces. Against whom is the God of the universe aroused to demonstrate such intense opposition? The proud. Do you want God to get his battle armor on? Be proud. Withdraw in pride. Attack in pride. Be "sweet" in pride. Lead in pride. God, help us!

We need God's help because although we are made in God's image, we are broken. Cheer up; we are worse than we think we are. We are the proud. The Greek word here carries with it a kind of self-deception. The word is: *huperephanos: hypér*, "beyond, over," and *phaínō*, "shine forth" – literally *over-shining*, trying to be *more* than we are. Pride is a distorted mirror, an in-your-dreams "*hyper-fantasy.*" It is NOT reality. God's light will show who we are.

Let's hear the warning, "God ***opposes*** the ***proud***."

Let's also hear the promise, "But shows favor to the humble." This favor is great – great enough to reconnect many with God and others. This favor is given through Jesus, and it is counterintuitive. Pastor and author Tim Keller writes,

> Many systems of thought appeal to strong, successful people, because they play directly into their belief that if you are strong and hardworking enough, you will prevail. But Christianity is ... for everyone, especially for people who admit that, where it really counts, they're weak. It is for people who have the particular kind of strength to admit that their flaws are not superficial, their heart is deeply disordered, and that they are incapable of rectifying

> themselves. It is for those who can see that they need a savior, that they need Jesus Christ dying on the cross, to put them right with God. [11]

Christian, cheer up; you are loved more than you can imagine.

Let's believe that grace can flow to us. Let's understand that grace flows downhill. Let's rejoice that God is looking for leaders in repentance. Jesus' FIRST message was: "Repent, the kingdom of heaven is near" (Mt. 4:17). Let's ask God to humble us by giving us the humility of Christ. Jesus says: "Take my yoke upon you, and learn from me, for I am gentle and *lowly* [the same Greek word translated *humble* in Peter and James] in heart, and you will find rest for your souls" (Matthew 11:29).

But, as you know, this promise of Jesus encounters a variety of challenges in our lives.

Our American way of living has fostered pride. Consider India and Mahatma Gandhi. When Gandhi was leading his people to independence and needed to travel by train, he chose the overcrowded third class car, with the poor, with animals. When asked why he traveled third class, he replied: "Because there is not a fourth class."

A preacher friend and his son traveled to India to meet an Indian pastor. The Indian pastor read 2 Corinthians 4:5: "For we do not preach ourselves, but Jesus Christ as Lord, and ourselves as your slaves for Jesus' sake." Then he asked the preacher:

- *"Do you preach yourself?"* My friend responded, *"I hope not."* We want to preach Christ and his Word. But, although we attempt that, we can still preach ourselves. We are tempted to preach our own agenda from the frame of reference we know best: ourselves. But God resists the proud.

- *"Do you preach Jesus Christ as Lord?"* He responded, "I hope so." If not, our churches become merely another kind of sociological phenomenon, like a club.

- *"Do you preach yourself as a slave to God's people for Jesus' sake?"* He said, "No, I do not." The Indian pastor replied, "You are right. No independent American would preach that he was a slave. Such humility is un-American."

When my friend told me that story, I pastored a church in an area known for having many Ph.Ds. I wondered: "God, could you help our church be known for humility, even in a proud place like this?" I knew it would not be wise to have a series of vision sermons on "Humility"; that would be like adding lemonade to a gas tank. So, I simply and regularly asked God to help me lead with humility. He did. I stepped back from some leadership. I delegated. I encouraged other leaders. Years later, a man who came to our church during that time told me he was attracted to our church because he saw humility among the leadership. I was astonished. God was not. "God shows favor to the humble."

General George Marshall (1880-1959) was chief of staff for the army during World War II. In 1953, he was awarded the Nobel Peace Prize for his Marshall Plan to rebuild war-torn Europe. Earlier in his career, in 1927, he had been appointed to command the infantry school at Fort Benning, Georgia. Paint peeled from the buildings; weeds grew on the grounds. Marshall could have been "large and in charge" and commanded that it be restored. Instead, he gathered paint, building supplies and gardening tools. Then, he began fixing up his personal quarters. As he painted, cleaned, trimmed, mowed and planted, the other men began doing the same. Within a few weeks, Fort Benning was transformed by the quiet, humble influence of General Marshall.

In our legislative, judicial, or executive branches, we are often part of a culture of pride. How counterintuitive to be countercultural and aim at humility!

Follow Colin Powell's advice. In essence, Powell has rephrased "God opposes the proud but shows favor to the humble" in these words:

- "The job of a leader is not to be the chief organizer, but the chief dis-organizer." You are not in the position God has given you to promote a system that perpetuates pride. You are there as a representative – primarily his representative – and he is humble.
- "Good leaders delegate and empower others liberally, but they pay attention to details, every day." That takes humility.
- "The day your people stop bringing you their problems is the day you have stopped leading them. They have either lost confidence that you can help them or concluded that you do not care. Real leaders are accessible and available." That takes humility.
- "Policies that emanate from ivory towers often have an adverse impact on the people out in the field who are fighting the wars or bringing in the revenues." Humility may be introverted, but it is not elitist and withdrawn.
- "Good leadership encourages everyone's evolution." Humility encourages growth. Pride stagnates while promising to change.
- "Keep looking below surface appearances. Don't shrink from doing so because you might not like what you find." Humility gets past superficiality because it lives in the real world.
- "Only by attracting the best people will you accomplish great deeds." Humility is not intimidated by the greatness of others; it seeks out that greatness.[12]

How do we connect with each other? Often it is through humility. Even – perhaps, especially – in proud places.

In the hallway of our state capitol, I bumped into a legislator I'll call "John." During the four months our legislature is in session, we have an early Thursday morning weekly Bible study. John attended that study. He and I had just started to get to know each other. He told me about a conversation he had with a representative I'll call "Paul," who was very discouraged. I asked John if Paul would like to attend the Thursday morning Bible study. John said, "My friend is not ready for that." I asked if I could take Paul out for coffee and listen. John thought that might be a possibility.

Later that day, I followed up by finding Paul's full name and email address. What follows is a series of communications that took place by email. Patiently work your way through them and note the reality of failed communication and the need for humility.

I wrote John, "I found Paul's email. Should I contact him? Would you prefer dropping him a note letting him know I'll be in touch?"

John replied, "Yep. His name is Paul." That was it - that was all John wrote. Since he did not answer my concern about contacting Paul without an introduction, what should I do? I decided to take action. I wrote the following email.

> Dear Paul, This morning, I ran into your friend John ____ (I'm copying him). In a general way, he told me that you'd had some discouraging times. I asked John if he thought you might like a cup of coffee - on me. He thought you might.
>
> I've lived here for 6 years. I'm called a pastor at large. In other words, I am not a lobbyist nor am I coming with a political agenda. Here are the kinds of questions I have:
>
> Who are you?
>
> What prompted you to run for office?

What are the important issues facing your constituents and state?

What do you like to read?

Is there any way I can encourage you?

So, if possible, I'm simply looking for ways to serve you - with your permission.

Late that night, John replied, "If you haven't sent this to Paul yet, let's talk first...just so I can protect his relationship with me. Thanks very much!"

My heart sank. I wrote back,

Dear John, Sorry to say, I did send it. I had asked if you wanted to introduce me to him. When you didn't respond to that email, I thought, "Well, I'll give it a try anyway." So, I was presumptuous and feel stupid. I hope you can forgive me. I'll pray that God will somehow use this for good.

John replied very late. "No problem...I'll catch up with him tomorrow and let him know who you are. Sorry I didn't read down the rest of the email. Was headed out in a rush. I noticed his email address was wrong so thought it might be undeliverable."

I wrote back, "Thanks - very much. God has great mercy. In my speed, as you noticed, I did mistype Paul's address. An email notifying me of my mistake just came. What a relief."

John replied,

God is good! Paul is really tight about giving any information to anyone, so I was concerned that a wedge might come between us. I sat down with him first thing this morning and told him what happened - so we're good. He got 1400 spam emails yesterday; he had given up and deleted the ones he couldn't get to. I'll introduce you to Paul on a casual note. God is good and his mercy endures forever!

My final reply was,

Thanks for sitting down with Paul first thing this morning. I didn't sleep too well last night. My worries prompted me to ask Jesus - several times - for his help. I never would have guessed it would have come this way. Thanks for your graciousness in all this.

Now, thank you for patiently reading through those emails. John and I went on to develop more of a friendship during the session. That would have been very difficult if humility was not evident from him – and from me.

And what is the source of that humility? To the extent that it is true humility, we believe Jesus is the source.

I've found help with humility from another group who knew Jesus well. During the mid-1600s, a large group of pastors and leaders asked questions about the nature of genuine authority. They searched the Bible for answers. For example, they asked: "As those who are under authority, what honor do we owe those in authority?" Among the answers they found were:

- praying and giving thanks for those in authority;
- imitating their virtues and graces;
- willingly obeying their legitimate commands, accepting their guidance, submitting to their corrections;
- remembering the nature of their positions;
- bearing with their weaknesses and covering them in love.[13]

They also asked: "What is required of those in authority towards those under their authority?" Among the answers they found were:

- to love, pray for, and bless those under their authority;

- to instruct, counsel, and admonish us: encouraging, commending, and rewarding those who do well; showing displeasure, reproving and correcting those who do not.
- to protect and provide for us in everything needed for soul and body.[14]

I love those answers. But I love something more. Before they answered the question above, they used a powerful qualifying phrase: "According to the power they receive from God." If those in authority are to lead well, they must depend upon God's help. Let's begin there too.

How do we receive power from God? We humbly pray and we humbly ask others to pray for us. May God raise up many who will respond like Samuel: "God forbid that I should sin against the LORD in ceasing to pray for you" (1 Sam 12:23). Let's pray and ask others to pray that God grants us the humility of Christ. "God opposes the proud but shows favor to the humble."

Your treadmill is calling. Has this essay helped you take a step toward humility?

We began with C. S. Lewis. Let's conclude with him: "There are only two kinds of people in the end: those who say to God, "Your will be done," and those to whom God says, in the end, "Your will be done." [15]

"Today, as then, those who rule are meant to rule with meekness. To be in a position of civil authority is to take seriously the obligations to and the cares of those we serve."

—Sen. Mark O. Hatfield, 1982

CHAPTER 6

INTRODUCTION TO CHRISTIAN SOCIAL ETHICS

DAVID CLYDE JONES

Christian ethics is the study of the way of life that conforms to the will of God. It concerns not only the personal virtues of the individual and interpersonal relationships between individuals, but also the social structures of human beings living in community, especially those institutions God has ordained with specific functions for the sake of human flourishing. These are principally marriage and the family, civil government, and the visible church institute.

A. The Rightful Exercise of Authority

> In the family of the just who live by faith and are as yet pilgrims journeying on to the celestial city, even those who rule serve those whom they seem to command; for they rule not from a love of power, but from a sense of the duty they owe to others—not because they are proud of authority, but because they love mercy.
>
> —St. Augustine, *The City of God*[16]

Historically the Christian tradition in ethics subsumes social structures under the commandment in the Decalogue: "Honor your father and your mother that your days may be long in the land which the LORD your God is giving you" (Ex 20:12). The underlying principle of the commandment appears to be *Respect for the rightful exercise of authority in divinely ordained social structures.* The argument goes like this.

Parents are God's representatives in the primary social unit, the marriage-based family (see Gn. 18:19; Dt. 6:4-7; Prov. 1:8, 6:20). Instruction of children in these texts is the joint responsibility of father and mother; Lv. 19:3 highlights respect for maternal authority by reversing the usual parental order: "Every one of you shall revere his mother and his father." The principle is eminently fulfilled in the example of Jesus: "And he went down with them [Mary and Joseph] and came to Nazareth and was submissive to them" (Lk 2:51). Rule in other spheres is similar. Elders in the apostolic church first earned respect as fathers (1 Tim 3:4-5). Deborah, the judge, is described as "a mother in Israel" (Jud 5:7). Peter extends the language of honor, that is, respect for lawful authority, to the emperor (1 Pet 2:17).

The Dutch theologian and ethicist J. Douma makes a double-edged point about the *rightful* exercise of authority: "Scripturally we must respect authority because it comes from God and people are clothed with authority by God." That's the one edge; this is the other (well-captured by Augustine in the epigraph above): "Authority is the authorization for the (appropriate) use of power. … Authority has a *serving* character. … It must be used for the honor of God and service of the neighbor."[17] Thus, on the one hand, the structural relationship by which some human beings have authority over others is divinely ordained; the rightfulness of the authority derives from the structure. On the other hand, the authority must be exercised rightfully, that is, in the manner and for the purposes that God intends. Institutional supra- and sub-ordination is a matter of divinely given responsibilities, not superior and inferior human beings. Authority is transformed by the Christian understanding of service following the example of Jesus (Mt 20:25-28; Jn 13:12-17).

B. The Dual Citizenship of Believers

As believers in the Lord Jesus Christ we are citizens of the heavenly Jerusalem.

> Our citizenship is in heaven, and from it we await a Savior, the Lord Jesus Christ.
>
> — Phil. 3:20; cf. Heb. 11:10; 12:22-24; Eph. 2:19; Ps. 87

At the same time, we continue to be citizens of some earthy polis.

> Only behave as citizens worthy of the gospel of Christ.
>
> —Phil. 1:27 mg; cf. Acts 16:35-40, 21:39, 22:25-29

We are visibly identified as members of the Christian faith community through baptism, the ordinance that marks our entrance into the visible church institute governed by pastors ("teaching and ruling elders" in Presbyterian polity). We are citizens of a particular civil society by birth or naturalization. Civil society is governed by magistrates ("princes" in the old terminology). The goal of church government is the discipleship of its members (Mt. 28:19-20); the goal of the civil government is to establish and maintain a just and tranquil social order (1 Tim. 2:2). The following schematic summarizes the relationship of believers to church and state:

Faith community ("the body of Christ")	Civil society ("the body politic")
• Members by baptism	• Citizens by birth or naturalization
• Governed by pastors	• Governed by magistrates
• Goal: discipleship of believers	• Goal: just and tranquil social order

The separation of powers according to their respective ends was admirably expressed by John of Damascus already in the eighth century:

> It does not belong to kings to legislate for the church … to kings belongs the maintenance of civil order, but the administration of the Church belongs to the shepherds and teachers. [18]

The essential theological framework within which the relationship between discipleship and citizenship has to be addressed is the nature of the present epoch in the history of redemption, the time between the Session of Jesus at God's right hand and his Second Coming in glory. The kingdom as both present and future is the indispensable biblical category for understanding the Christian calling as citizens of the heavenly Jerusalem living on earth as the visible church of the Lord Jesus, called to responsible participation in the civil society of which by God's providence they are a vital part. As the late Ed Clowney commented on the social contribution of Christians, "The renewal of life in Christ makes the people of God to be a leaven in the culture of this world. Like salt they preserve the world from further corruption. The light of their renewed understanding influences the thinking and actions of men around them."[19]

The diagram below is intended to express the dynamics of the present stage of the coming of the kingdom as believers work out their discipleship in responsible citizenship, the goal of which is social transformation for the common good. Such transformation has three components, the first of which is *personal renewal* since character formation in the image of Christ is at the root of everything else. The second component is *ecclesial practice* since the church as a corporate body should provide a model of what living in community according to the will of God should look like. The third component is *structural reform* of institutions that are marred by sin. This is the special responsibility of those for whom politics is a divine calling. The large circle below represents the social arena; the small circle is the visible church institute, from which believers emerge to pursue their various cultural callings.

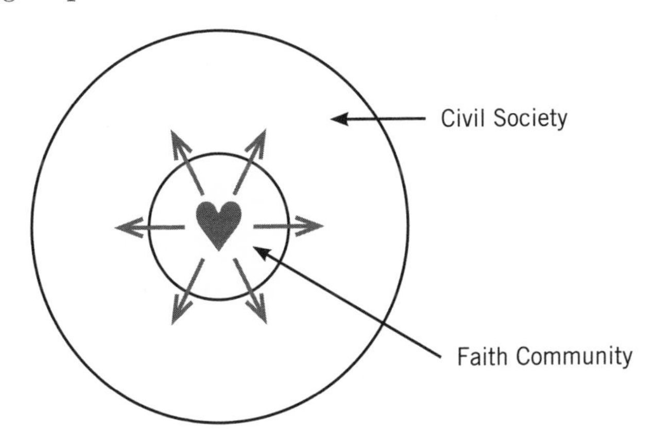

C. The Principle of Sphere Sovereignty

Sphere sovereignty is one of the ideas that have emerged from "the seedbed Christian tradition," along with the rule of law, constitutionalism, division of powers, the inviolability of the human person, and natural human rights, especially of the poor (not to deny that these have other roots as well).[20]

The development of a world-and-life view structured around the principle of sphere sovereignty is arguably the most significant contribution of the Calvinist tradition to Western culture formation.

The idea is that God has built into the world a diversity of cultural spheres—political, scientific, artistic, familial, educational, economic, and so forth—that God intends to be developed by human beings according to the original "cultural mandate" given to the human race at creation. Sin, however, has distorted the development of the cultural spheres. The task of redeemed humanity is to reclaim all spheres of life for the glory of God, not by imposing an official theocratic control on human cultural explorations, but by establishing God-honoring cultural projects and institutions to counter the corrupt manifestations of sinful cultural formation.

How does this relate to the coming of the kingdom? According to Princeton theologian Geerhardus Vos, "Whenever one of these spheres comes under the controlling influence of the principle of divine supremacy and glory, and this outwardly reveals itself, there we can truly say that the kingdom of God has become manifest."[21] Note that each sphere is ordained by God with its own proper aims and its own unique patterns of authority.

Adding the names of representative cultural spheres to our church and society diagram yields the following result:

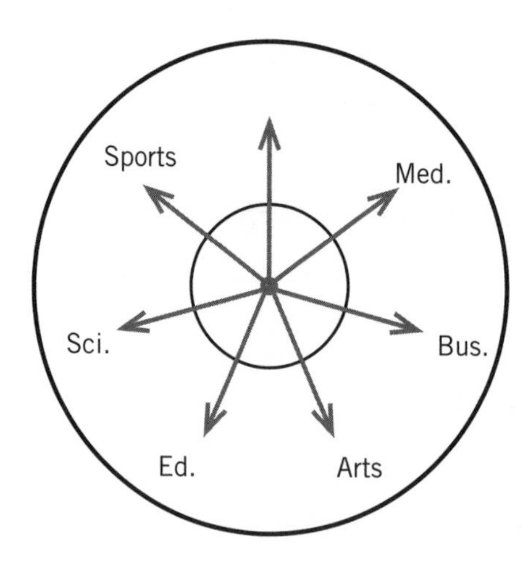

There are a couple of observations to be made concerning this scheme for developing a Christian social philosophy. First, the cultural mandate is the common calling of humankind, believers and non-believers alike. The breakout contribution of Abraham Kuyper was his recognition of the possibility of authentic Christian action in the domain of common grace in cooperation with non-believers. This paved the way for cooperative cultural endeavors in civil society for the common good irrespective of ultimate worldview commitments.

Secondly, although the state governs civil society as a whole, it "takes its place not *above* all other spheres, but rather next to them. Its high and overarching position is due not to a natural hierarchy but to the state's peculiar character as *public* authority."[22] Its sphere of responsibility is to ensure the social conditions of justice and peace that allow all the other spheres to fulfill their specific purpose for human flourishing. The Reformed principle of *sphere sovereignty* is paralleled in the Roman Catholic principle of *subsidiarity* which specifies that "A community of a higher order in society should not assume tasks belonging to a community of lower order and deprive it of its authority."

Perhaps this rude diagram will help to visualize how the principle of sphere sovereignty operates. Note that the church is part of civil society and the state exists alongside, not above, the other spheres.

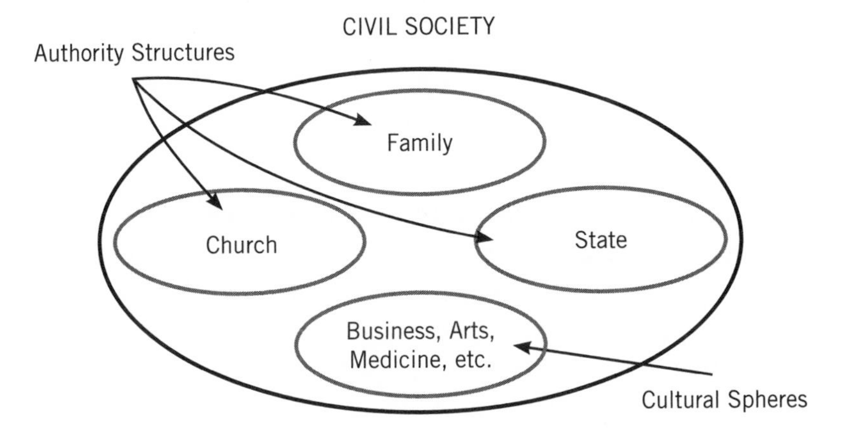

D. Religion and Politics

The institutional separation of church and state, or more precisely, the separation of the *government of faith communities* from the *government of civil society*, is a separation devoutly to be wished. But that is not at all the same thing as the separation of religion and politics. The separation of church and state is highly desirable; the separation of religion and politics is simply impossible. Why is that? Because politics is the domain of public policy, and public policy proposals are inevitably the expression of some world-and-life view, some conception of the common good to be aimed at for human beings living in community. Public policy proposals are worldview dependent, and worldviews, theistic and non-theistic, are religious in nature as ultimate faith commitments.

This is especially important for the principle of sphere sovereignty sketched above. Not only are the governing authorities of church and state distinct, but also participation in the cultural spheres is religious activity on the part of believers just as much as their corporate worship and diaconal ministries in the visible church institute. That all of life is religious in this sense is important for understanding the full meaning of religious liberty. The idea of freedom of religious faith and practice was a long time in coming in political philosophy and remains a matter of controversy down to the present day. The main competing visions of the relationship between religion and society as they developed historically are territorialism, non-establishmentarianism, and secular monism.

1. Territorialism

Territorialism refers to the territorial coincidence of a particular religion and society. It was the assumption of the Old Testament theocracy, whether ruled by judges or kings, and it became the assumption of Christendom after the conversion of the emperor Constantine (with the concurrence of Augustine who approved civil punishment of heretics and schismatics).

Take France as an example. The "most Christian king," Francis I, swore in his coronation oath that he would not tolerate heretics in his realm. Calvin's first edition of the *Institutes* (1536) was written to convince the king that "Lutherans" (aka evangelicals or protestants or reformed or, in France, Huguenots) were not heretics. The king was persecuting the wrong people. The common ground was captured in the slogan *un roi, une loi, une foi* (one king, one law, one faith); the ruler or "prince" had the duty to establish the faith and to impose legislation accordingly.

The territorial assumption was "Remove religion and you dissolve the bonds that hold civil society together" (André Maillard to Henry IV of France). Thus, when Jeanne d'Albret, Queen of Navarre, publicly converted to the Reformed faith in 1560, Calvin urged her to follow through with establishment of the Reformed religion. "I know the arguments advanced to prove that princes should not force their subjects to lead a Christian life ... but all kingdoms which do not serve that of Jesus Christ are ruined, so judge for yourself."[23]

In September 1563, Pope Pius IV condemned Jeanne for heresy and summoned her to appear before the Inquisition in Rome within six months. She wisely declined. In February 1564, Jeanne issued an edict permitting Mass in places where it was currently celebrated, an early example of tolerance within a single kingdom. Eventually she acted on Calvin's advice and issued the following proclamation:

> Jeanne, by the grace of God, Queen of Navarre, Sovereign Lady of Béarn ...
>
> To all present and to come: health and joy.
>
> There is no monarch alive who is not obligated to use his full powers to place his subjects under the rule of Jesus Christ ...

> In order, therefore, to obey the Lord's commandment, to fulfill the obligations of a Christian, to respond to the vocation given us by God, to procure the salvation of our subjects, to assure the unity of our administration and of the public peace ... it is our will that all subjects ... of whatever quality, condition, or estate, shall profess publicly the Confession of Faith [The Confession of La Rochelle, affirmed by representatives of the French Reformed churches in Navarre, Geneva, and France, April 1571] that we here publish by our authority as surely founded on the doctrine and writings of the Prophets and of the Apostles.[24]

The conception of society common to Catholics and Calvinists in the 16th century was *monistic*; the faith community (visible church) and the political community (nation or city-state) were *coextensive*. Baptism signified membership in both church and state. (This was the driving principle behind the persecution of the Anabaptists. Denial of the Trinity and the practice of repeat baptism were capital crimes throughout Christendom; Servetus was found guilty on both counts.)

The theological crisis of the 16th century was addressed by the Peace of Augsburg (1555) on the principle *cuis regio, eius religio* (whose region, his religion). All parties accepted this proposition: "Church membership was coterminous and interchangeable with territorial location, and territorial rule was established on, and made legitimate by, the ruler's professed religion."[25] A contemporary example is the Islamist vision: "Restoration of a unified worldwide political community, the *ummah*, ruled by a centralized Islamic authority, the caliphate, governed by a reactionary version of Islamic law, *shari'a.*" [26]

2. Non-establishmentarianism

At the founding of the American republic, the political community ("We the people") through its appointed representatives opted for non-discrimination on the basis of religion for full citizen participation in the government of civil society:

> [Officials of all branches of government] shall be bound by oath or affirmation to support this Constitution; but no religious test shall ever be required as a qualification to any office or public trust under the United States.[27]

The principle was reiterated as the first freedom enumerated in the Bill of Rights: "*Congress* shall make no law respecting an establishment of religion or prohibiting the free exercise thereof."[28]

Presbyterians were a major voice for religious freedom at the founding. A memorial of the Presbyterians of Virginia, August 13, 1785, declared, "The end of civil government is security to the temporal liberty and property of mankind, and to protect them in the free exercise of religion." While the Constitution was in process of being ratified by the States, the Presbyterian Church amended its doctrinal standards and Book of Church Order ("tolerating a false religion" was deleted from the list of sins forbidden in the Larger Catechism, q. 109, although the proposition that the church should be "*countenanced and maintained by the civil magistrate*" was left intact, q. 275). The 1788 Form of Government and Discipline stated in its opening paragraph:

> God alone is Lord of the conscience ... the rights of private judgment, in all matters that respect religion, [are] universal and inalienable. [We] do not even wish to see any religious constitution aided by the civil power, further than may be necessary for protection and security, and, at the same time, equal and common to all others.[29]

More recently the Roman Catholic Church has altered its position on religious freedom in its landmark *Declaration on Religious Freedom* (*Dignitatis humanae personae*) promulgated by Vatican II, 1965. The argument is that coercion in religion is fundamentally opposed to the dignity of the human person. The theologian more responsible than any other for *Dignitatis humanae* was the American Jesuit John Courtney Murray, whose treatise *We Hold These Truths: Catholic Reflections on the American Proposition* (1960) is a classic presentation of the constellation of ideas that undergird the American experiment:

> …that government has a moral basis; that the universal moral law is the foundation of society; that the legal order of society—that is, the state—is subject to judgment by a law that is not statistical but inherent in the nature of man; that the eternal reason of God is the ultimate origin of all law; that this nation in all its aspects—as a society, a state, and ordered and free relationship between governors and governed—is under God. [30]

These propositions, Murray argues, are more the product of Christian history than a piece of 18th century rationalist theory. It is that history which eventuated in the idea of a pluralistic civil society in the following sense:

> By pluralism … I mean the coexistence within the one political community of groups who hold divergent and incompatible views with regard to religious questions—those ultimate questions that concern the nature and destiny of man within a universe that stands under the reign of God.[31]

The practical consequences of this conception of a religiously pluralistic society were immediately observable at the founding as Jews and Christians marched arm in arm in the Grand Federal

Procession in Philadelphia on the occasion of the ratification of the Constitution by the State of Pennsylvania in 1788. As President Washington wrote to the Hebrew Congregation at New Port, Rhode Island, in 1790, "The citizens of the USA have ... given to mankind examples of an enlarged and liberal policy ... All possess a like liberty of conscience and immunities of citizenship."

3. Secular monism

> Separating the institutions of church and state does not mean separating the religious conscience from politics.[32]

I think it was Jean Bethke Elshtain who first used the term *monism* to describe the school of thought that "holds that when religious persons enter the public sphere they are obliged to do so in a secular civic idiom short of any explicit reference to religious commitment and belief."[33] The bright line of separation between church and state as authority structures with distinct social roles is extended to religion and politics generally. "Thus, in the name of neutrality, this school actually imposes one framework as 'the American way.'"

The late Cardinal Bernadin enumerated three ways religion necessarily has a public role: (1) articulation of a consistent ethic of life; (2) contribution to civil society through faith-based institutions in education, health-care, family services, and outreach to the poorest in society; (3) character formation, teaching service of neighbor and civic stewardship. The introduction of religiously grounded moral belief into public policy proposals does not violate the disestablishment principle. As Michael J. Perry observes, "Because of the role that religiously grounded moral belief inevitably plays in the political process ... it is important that such beliefs, no less than secular moral beliefs, be presented in public political argument so that they can be tested there."[34]

Ministry to State?

Why should we have such a work as Ministry to State?

That's a good question. The intrinsic logic of the cultural mandate is that *all* vocations are to be pursued Christianly and should be developed by those in the various spheres by applying the word of God to their specific callings themselves, thus avoiding clerical dominance. Isn't that principle in conflict with a special ministry to *state* and not business, or medicine, or one of any number of spheres?

Not necessarily, in my opinion. The key is construal in terms of *ministry* rather than any kind of authoritative oversight. The rationale for special ministry to those in civil government is their special role in the government of civil society, a role that directly affects everyone and presents particular temptations for "selling out" one's convictions in the pursuit of power and yielding to the temptation to the abuse of power once it is obtained.

I think no one has captured this better than Martin Franzmann, whom I had the privilege of studying under in graduate school. Franzmann published a little collection of prayers titled *Pray for Joy* (Concordia, 1970), one of which was "For Charity Toward Men in Office." It contains these pertinent lines:

O God, remember in Your mercy

> the men who bear the burden of this majesty,
> men like us, easily bent
>
> > by the pressure of temptation,
> > by the impact of expediency.

Remember them and strengthen them when they are moved

> to shade the truth to their own ends,
> to withhold what should be told,
> to distort what must be told,

to disclose what does not serve our common
weal.

Keep intact their honor and their credibility.[35]

CHAPTER 7

THE LEADERSHIP INTERSECTION AND INTERDEPENDENCY OF CHURCH & STATE

HARRY REEDER

After reading the magisterial American Declaration of Independence, the English parliamentarian Horace Walpole is quoted as remarking, "Cousin America has run off with a Presbyterian parson." Walpole's purpose of diminishing and mocking the proclamation was, at least momentarily, achieved. Despite the derogatory intent, the comment was quite revelatory as to the origin, energy and framing of the Declaration and the soon-to-follow documents of American national law, the Constitution and the astonishing Bill of Rights.

Much of the 18th century's inexorable movement to independence, national sovereignty and representative democracy, with primacy of law, in the American colonies was indebted emotionally, spiritually and conceptually to the evangelical church in general, and to the Great Awakening in particular. The separation of church and state, suggested in embryonic form at Geneva during the Reformation, the publication of Samuel Rutherford's *Lex, Rex* ("Law is King"), and the preaching of George Whitefield and others provided impetus for the American pursuit of independence. Walpole's statement encapsulated the role of the church in producing the American movement to independence. But it also included a very specific and personal observation: There actually was a Presbyterian pastor who prominently influenced the independence movement and its documents, including the Declaration of Independence, the Constitution and the Bill of Rights.

In the Continental Congress, thirteen delegates were either formally or informally led or mentored by the Presbyterian minister, Jonathan Witherspoon, who also presided over Princeton College. James Madison, a key participant in the important decisions of the day and chief architect of the Constitution, was a friend and student of Witherspoon's. The Witherspoon connections and influence extended throughout the Continental Congress and beyond into the lives of the legal, ecclesiastical and cultural thinkers and leaders of the fledgling nation. But such Christian ministerial engagement and influence went way beyond Witherspoon.

The careful, thoughtful, and persistent influence of John Adams, an energetic and highly committed Christian, encouraged and assisted the prolific and equally energetic Thomas Jefferson, keeping him from some of the excesses of his libertarian bent and fascination with the doomed concepts of liberty without law, as embraced by the French Revolution and its inevitable anarchy. In addition, Benjamin Franklin, at best a Deist, was without doubt influenced by the preaching, counsel and friendship of the great evangelist and American independence supporter George Whitefield. The relentless preaching and publications of the pastor/evangelist Samuel Davies would be impossible to measure as a factor in the formation of public policy, influence upon public leaders, and, therefore, the direction of this new country. Through these men and others, we see the concept clearly articulated that the church was not to rule the state and the state was not to rule over or through the church. In other words, the church and the state were connected organically but not organizationally. The profitable nature of this dynamic relationship, when properly enacted, provides almost limitless benefit.

We are all aware of the statesmanship exhibited by William Wilberforce, who with steadfastness stayed the course of 28 years to eradicate slavery without a war in the British Empire. Not as many of us are aware of the believers, including John Newton, the former slave trader, then preacher, theologian, pastor and hymnist, who encouraged and pastored Wilberforce to the excellent victory. So what are the implications and lessons to state/government leaders whom the Lord identifies as His ministers "to affirm righteousness and punish evildoers"? And what does this mean to Christians in general and church leaders in particular as to how they are to participate in the public square and even more pointedly in the formation and implementation of public theology with beneficial public policies?

Leaders who do what is needed for their generation and for the generations to come are essential. Such leaders must be intentionally developed and deployed from the church into the world with gospel-driven character and biblically-informed concepts of public policy and the necessary competencies to lead with principled effectiveness. These statesmen-leaders normally come by way of God's grace at work through gospel-saturated evangelism and discipleship. In addition, other gifted leaders who are unbelievers are shaped and made beneficial to the public by the influence of God's people as salt and light in the culture. The church of Jesus Christ has a God-given responsibility to pursue not only the gospel ministry of redeeming grace but also the ministry of public blessing through common grace from the pulpit to the pew and into the community, as the gospel of grace is proclaimed in word and displayed in deed.

When God's covenant people embrace their responsibilities to speak to matters of public theology, influencing and producing leaders for the state, humanity benefits greatly. When the commitment to being an instrument of common grace in public policy and producing statesmen leaders is neglected or rejected, then the culture suffers. The church can fulfill its Great Commission responsibilities while shepherding the flock of God and prophetically speaking to matters of public theology, while simultaneously developing and deploying Christian statesmen. History is replete with both the blessings of the church's multi-faceted ministry efforts and the curses resulting from the church's silence and withdrawal from the public square of governmental engagement. These cursed results have led not merely to social discomfort and chaos but, sadly, even to the wholesale loss of life.

What would have happened if the evangelical church and its extraordinarily gifted leaders and preachers, particularly in the South, had addressed the issues of chattel slavery by providing leaders and policies to eradicate legalized man-stealing, which is clearly condemned in the Scripture? Could 700,000 casualties, countless fatherless homes, and husbandless marriages have been avoided? What would have happened in Germany if the confessing church had spoken up when the trains filled with Jews headed to concentration camps passed by their churches?

History and Scripture record multiple moments when God's people benefited society by engaging in matters of public policy and providing effective public servants. Here is one such moment, briefly considered, from the life and protracted ministry of Daniel, supported by his three colleagues popularly known by their Babylonian names of Shadrach, Meshach and Abednego.

But first a biblical parameter needs to be stated: God's Word does not allow us to be passive when it comes to living out our lives in this world. Our Savior instructed us to be "in the world" but not "of the world." In other words, while we are to be "in the world" we are not to live in a way that allows the world into us. Leaders in local, state and national arenas live and work in environments that are not gospel-friendly, and in some situations are demonstrably adversarial. All of our elected and appointed leaders need the church to graciously and authentically interact with them as salt and light. To both speak truth to them faithfully and love them relentlessly is crucial. How would this look if done well? Let's consider the life of Daniel.

Daniel understood how to live in a pagan culture as a leader, developer of leaders, and counselor to the most important rulers in the world. Amazingly, as he did all of this, he simultaneously demonstrated the saving and life-changing power of God's grace. Daniel's leadership had such an unbelievably prolonged influence that, like Joseph, another public servant who blessed both believers and non-believers, nothing negative is said about him in the Scriptures.

In the first chapter of the book of Daniel, set in 605 B.C., Nebuchadnezzar had defeated the king of Judah, Jehoiakim. He decided not to bring him back as a prisoner, but instead to bring back the captured vessels of the Temple and, more importantly, some choice youths for a very specific purpose. This decision eventually placed Daniel and his companions in positions of leadership and influence for an 80-year period.

Babylon was to have a long history as an empire and would be used clearly for God's purposes. One of the multiple prophetic statements of why God raised up Babylon is found in the book of Chronicles. The chronicler records that because King Jehoiakim had done what was evil in the sight of God, judgment would come upon him. King Nebuchadnezzar would eventually destroy the Temple in 586 B.C., again fulfilling biblical prophecy. His first religious statement was removal of the vessels of the Temple to Babylon.

Along with the judgment upon King Jehoiakim, something else was happening in God's sovereign plan. It began with King Nebuchadnezzar taking young leaders from the prominent families of the people whom he had defeated:

> Then the king commanded Ashpenaz, his chief eunuch, to bring some of the people of Israel, both of the royal

> family and of the nobility, youths without blemish, of good appearance and skillful in all wisdom, endowed with knowledge, understanding learning, and competent to stand in the king's palace, and to teach them the literature and language of the Chaldeans. The king assigned them a daily portion of the food that the king ate, and of the wine that he drank. They were to be educated for three years, and at the end of that time they were to stand before the king. Among these were Daniel, Hananiah, Mishael, and Azariah of the tribe of Judah. And the chief of the eunuchs gave them names: Daniel he called Belteshazzar, Hananiah he called Shadrach, Mishael he called Meshach, and Azariah he called Abednego. –Daniel 1: 3-7, ESV

King Nebuchadnezzar had very definite ideas about leadership and leadership development, which in some ways were not unlike our ideas today. He wanted these four men, among others not identified, to be assimilated into the Chaldean culture and into his aristocracy. He programmed his intent to paganize them.

- Step one was to remove their Hebrew names and give them pagan names as their primary identity.
- Step two was to put them in a three-year pagan school to teach them the sophistication of the prevailing pagan world and life views.
- Step three was to make them participate in a pagan diet including, and focused upon, the king's table.

Daniel, the soon-to-be acknowledged wise man, now at this tender age showed the God-given and Scripture-shaped "wisdom from above." Daniel's ability to discern and wisely navigate this difficult circumstance in a manner that would leave him both faithful to God and able to influence the public and private policy of the king is instructive and inspiring. From this event we are given important insights regarding effective and influential leadership lived with biblical world and life views.

It was not sinful (i.e., transgressing God's law) for Daniel or his friends to be given pagan names. Nor was it sinful for them to be exposed to the elements of a Babylonian education. But Daniel and his companions knew that to eat from the king's table would cross the line, in that it would require them to transgress God's law. The fact that the table was furnished with wine and meat was not the problem, since both wine and meat were permissible in the diet of a Jew. But the Old Testament clearly stated that God's people were not to defile themselves with anything which had been offered to idols. The king's table was, by definition, a feast dedicated to some pagan deity, and the meat that was eaten and even, perhaps, the wine drunk, had been dedicated, sacrificed and consecrated to the deity. So with the prohibitions of Leviticus and Exodus in Daniel's mind, he knew he could not disobey God's revealed will. What is also clear is that Daniel did not draw a line. God had drawn the line, so Daniel put his life on the line that God had drawn. This reveals the character of Daniel and his friends, and we see a profile of leadership that is desperately needed today. The Scripture opens the door for us to gain crucial insights into this leadership portrait:

> But Daniel resolved that he would not defile himself with the king's food, or with the wine that he drank. Therefore he asked the chief of the eunuchs to allow him not to defile himself. And God gave Daniel favor and compassion in the sight of the chief of the eunuchs, and the chief of the eunuchs said to Daniel, "I fear my lord the king, who assigned your food and your drink; for why should he see that you were in worse condition than the youths who are of your own age? So you would endanger my head with the king?" Then Daniel said to the steward whom the chief of the eunuchs had assigned over Daniel,

> Hananiah, Mishael, and Azariah, "Test your servants for ten days; let us be given vegetables to eat and water to drink. Then let our appearance and the appearance of the youths who eat the king's food be observed by you, and deal with your servants according to what you see." So he listened to them in this matter, and tested them for ten days. At the end of ten days it was seen that they were better in appearance and fatter in flesh than all the youths who ate the king's food. So the steward took away their food and the wine they were to drink, and gave them vegetables. –Daniel 1:8-16, ESV

Daniel responded to his dilemma with a proposed solution which is noticeably void of self-aggrandizement, arrogance, or self-righteousness. It is thoughtful, courageously humble and winsome. The proposal and its delivery are instructive for the following reasons.

1. The king had decreed something, making it law in terms of what Daniel was required to do. To reject and disobey the king's law was punishable by death. Daniel would have heard of King Nebuchadnezzar's "fiery furnace" and den of lions. They were not hidden but displayed publicly with full awareness that the king would use them freely upon any and all disobedient citizens.

2. Daniel was likely under intense peer pressure. Besides Shadrach, Meshach and Abednego, no other youths within the captivity had stood with Daniel and his friends, to our knowledge. Their colleagues in captivity were, as far as we can tell, engaging in the king's program. While friends and compatriots were defiling themselves, the four youths stood firm, despite peer pressure.

3. They had to know that death was assured if they did not comply and the king did not agree to their proposal. They

also knew about the fiery furnace and the lion's den, both of which they later faced.

4. They knew why they had been brought to Babylon. Any future opportunity for position, power and possessions was now at risk; in fact, having a future at all was at risk. If Daniel went along with the king's program, a wide door would open. Pragmatism would beckon them to "go along to get along." Would not compliance probably position them under Nebuchadnezzar to gain opportunities and power to help their people? All one had to do was simply go along and defile oneself. Wouldn't it be okay to disobey God's Word concerning ceremonial defilement in order to gain an influential position? This not only would be good for family, but would also help take care of his people at a later date. Daniel said "no" to the pragmatic notion that "ends justify the means," because the reality is that the means always determine the true end.

5. There was also the subtle but almost irresistible attraction of the unknown. Daniel, Shadrach, Meshach and Abednego had not grown up with the king's food and wine. It had to be, to them, a novelty. Why not just this one time gain a taste of the world and a seat at the table?

6. Another factor might have been the curiosity of what it would be like to try what always had been forbidden. Parents, with all the cultural and familial restraints, were hundreds of miles away in Israel. Could not Daniel and his friends be permitted, just this once, the allowance of sowing their wild oats and taking advantage of what they never could have experienced back home? Who would tell on them? To put it in today's terms, there were no cell phones. There was no email. They were isolated and alone, so who could know, or who would care? Yet Daniel

and his companions knew that they were always in the presence of God as they made their decisions for life.

7. Finally, might not Daniel be understandably disgruntled and ready to comply in self-pity and/or anger against God in light of his present condition of captivity? Would it not be permissible for him to say to himself, "I think I'll just go ahead and do this. God, look what you let them do to me. You let these people come and take me away from my family and my home, and if You are going to be that way to me, then watch what I do now that I am here."

Instead of letting his heart bow to a pagan decree, he purposed not to defile himself out of devotion to God.

It is not too much to assume that Daniel and his companions were granted wisdom from above, nor is it too much to assume that the Holy Spirit was using deposits which had been invested in their minds and hearts prior to their deportation. Long before this moment of trial, there had been the divinely-prescribed synergy of parents who raised their children to know the Word of God in order to know the God of the Word intimately and accurately. This would enable their covenant children to serve the Lord principally and passionately, as well as faithfully and effectively. These parents would have made full use of the divinely-provided means of grace within the covenant community, producing a pattern of leadership in their sons which would affect empires and dynasties for decades and echo through the corridors of time even to this day, by God's grace and for His glory.

Daniel humbly approached Ashpenaz with his courageous, thoughtful and God-reliant proposal, standing his ground in not partaking of wine or the meat from sacrifices, but showing flexibility in his willingness to eat vegetables and drink water at the king's table.

A leader needs to learn where to stand by identifying biblically what is non-negotiable and what is. While we have no ability to address the family backgrounds of our elected and appointed leaders, we can provide committed and competent models and mentors from the church who can disciple and pray with them, as well as for them, as they prepare to stand firm and negotiate with honor.

Disregarding the Word of God is never an option for Christians in leadership. They find out where God has drawn the line, and they faithfully step up to it. As they fearlessly stand on God's line, they are able to offer negotiated solutions which are reasonable, thoughtful, creative, kind and gracious. Observe not only the boldness of Daniel's stand, but also his graciousness and creativity in approaching Ashpenaz. He understood fear of the king, as all operated under threat of death. He also understood the difficulty of the situation, and therefore, offered a well-considered solution which did not fall short of God's Word, but also did not arrogantly exceed God's Word. It was a solution reliant upon God's faithfulness, revealing their allegiance to the Lord their God, yet honoring those in authority over them.

Christian boldness and conviction when displayed must always be accompanied by discernment and understanding, and firmly distanced from arrogance and self-righteousness. It is good and right to manifest a willingness to cooperate with others without compromising biblical standards and then deliver such solutions with a gentle clarity. That's what Daniel brought to the king's table and the moments of crisis. Not known at the time was that Daniel actually had set the table for future influence upon King Nebuchadnezzar, arguably leading even to his conversion, as recorded in later chapters.

The church cannot be passive and simply play the critic. We must define God-glorifying, Christ-centered, Holy-Spirit-reliant, Bible-shaped and gospel-driven leadership, develop leaders, and deploy them into every sphere of life. The church should become a leadership factory. By God's grace the church must make, multiply, and mobilize nation-shaking leaders who extend the kingdom of God from the colony of the kingdom, His church. The moment is now because the need is now and the Great Commandment is for now.

The gospel of Christ, which is the only answer to the cultural and spiritual entropy of this age, is to be delivered from our Lord's church in redeeming grace through evangelism and discipleship, enveloped by protracted intercessory prayer. This must be joined to the overflow of God's common grace though principled leaders with godly character, who know the Word of God with wisdom from God. Leaders must know their craft of godly public policy, and know how to deliver it with creative yet principled governance propelled by the love of Christ and drenched with a love for people made in the image of God.

The answer to sin and depravity throughout our nation will not originate from Pennsylvania Avenue, Wall Street, Market Street, Main Street, School House Lane, Hollywood Boulevard, Court House Square, or the capitols of states and nations. It will only originate from Church Street, the earthly capitol of the kingdom of God, having been sent from the King of Kings who reigns in heaven with all authority. Then prayerfully and thoughtfully it must be delivered to every street in the nation, with leaders who have been gospel-nurtured in the church and their families. This life-changing gospel answer is then delivered to and through Pennsylvania Avenue, Wall Street, Market Street, Main Street, School House Lane, Hollywood Boulevard, or Court House Square for the glory of God and the exaltation of Christ, displaying joyfully the grace of God to all so that all might be drawn to the Lord of glory.

CHAPTER 8

NONPARTISAN MINISTRY IN A HYPER-PARTISAN WORLD

BOBBY GRIFFITH

Life in the United States is marked by a growing Left-Right divide in which one must choose sides. "Do you watch Fox News?" Or, "You watch Fox news!?!?!?" "How can you stomach MSNBC?" "Why don't you watch MSNBC?" Our hyped, 24-hour news cycle thrives on controversies that highlight cultural or political differences. Conservatives have their causes. Liberals theirs. Those to the left, right or in-between have numerous causes as well.

Churches and denominations are expected to fall within those lines. Recently, a United Methodist minister was defrocked for performing a gay wedding. Famously, the Southern Baptists boycotted Disney. The United Church of Christ adopted the comma as a logo to say people should not put periods where God allows for commas, meaning that faith adapts to new social and political thinking.

The reality is that everyone has political commitments to some degree. In the U.S., Christian ministers are voices for both the Left and the Right. When a prominent pastor, aligned with the

Republican Party, weighs in on an issue, one is sure to hear Jim Wallis's take shortly thereafter. Some Christians vote based on Focus on the Family voter guides without researching issues themselves. Where do they find these guides? In their local churches, of course.

When I began ministering to the Oklahoma capitol community, I committed to minister winsomely. The Ministry to State handout that attendees use to invite friends states that *our only agenda is to love and serve the capitol*. We also make it known that we are nonpartisan. For a pastor, in Oklahoma, ordained in a denomination known for conservatism, this can be a tall order.

Why? Oklahoma is the state with a Ten Commandments monument. Oklahoma was the reddest state in the 2008 presidential election and second reddest in 2012. Both branches of state government are under the control of one party. Oklahoma has "open carry" gun laws, strict alcohol regulations, immigration laws that have been dismantled by the federal judiciary, and a pending bill that will make it illegal to ban "Merry Christmas." Noted political scientist Alan Hertzke affirms that "religion" plays an important role in the political realities of Oklahoma.

With all of that, how does one create nonpartisan space where Christians of differing political commitments can come together? This question is important because not all Christians share the same political views, and because Christians can be so committed to a political ideology that they do not realize that their offense lies not in the gospel, but politics. Capitols are symbols of power and policy and there is a great need for pastors to enter that arena. But, somehow, they must check their own ideology at the door without compromising their theological or political commitments.

I believe this can be done if one considers the historical, global, social and gospel contexts. Only then can we realize that our own political views are influenced by the weight of history, our local context and our own temporal milieu.

Historical Context

In the early 1990s, noted sociologist James Davison Hunter popularized the term "culture war." He argued that the intensification of secularism within the United States had given rise to political and social boundaries that deemphasized denominational divides and centered on cultural ones. Hunter looked at shifts in the 1960s, 1970s and 1980s, where issues surrounding the concepts of family and gender heightened cultural clashes. These conflicts were political, religious, and class-based, and divided along educational lines. Abortion, gay rights, feminism, the Equal Rights Amendment and other newer political and cultural shifts awakened traditionally-minded religious groups to speak out publically. In Hunter's view, a reactionary conservatism emerged that sees the family unit under attack and responds to preserve what Christopher Lasch called "a haven in a heartless world."

While the notion of culture war is a newer label in American vernacular, it is helpful to note that Christians have historically been divided politically.

During the American Revolution, many Christians held opposing political views. In fact, the Anglican Church rebranded as the Episcopal Church to avoid association with the British monarchy. While some pastors preached the "sacred cause of liberty," others gave impassioned pleas to be true to the crown.

Christians have been on differing sides in debates over free silver, taxes, free trade versus tariffs, prohibition of alcohol, women's rights, child labor laws, welfare, the New Deal, and the list goes on and on. While in retrospect we view issues like racism, slavery, and the treatment of women and children, and wonder, "How did they believe that?" we are more ambivalent on other issues, like silver and monetary policy. But Christians sharply disagreed at the time.

Even during the long Civil Rights struggle, Christians divided. Denominational leaders and presidents of Christian colleges touted theologies of segregation. At the same time, other

Christians vehemently opposed these views. Both sides made political claims alongside their theological ones. Christians were at the forefront of civil rights, abolition and other movements that reshaped U.S. history.

Even today, some Christians are incredulous that others disagree on certain political or cultural issues. Some voices in 2008 and 2012 stated that one could not be a Christian and vote for Barack Obama. Others opposed George W. Bush because of his handling of the war on terror, use of torture, or other issues.

How can we minister to state officials? Can a Presbyterian Republican minister to Democratic politicians? Can a Democratic Baptist share a meal with Republican staffers and pray with them?

The answer is yes!

Global Context

Throughout the world, Christians have wildly different political views. When I was in seminary, I asked my neighbor, a South Korean, "Do Koreans like President Bush?" He laughed and said "No." He then expressed his frustration with "American Christians" and their willingness to so easily support war. He said many of his fellow Korean Presbyterians could not believe some of the political issues American evangelicals supported. Since that conversation, I've had the privilege of studying history as a master of arts and doctoral student. It has been quite eye opening.

Globally, Christians do not see the world in a Left-Right divide. In England, you are likely to find MPs of all political stripes in the Church of England. We might cynically doubt their commitment, but the reality of their faith is between them, God and the Church. At a recent conference, Dr. Ligon Duncan recalled his surprise when, as a doctoral student in Scotland, he learned that believers in the theologically conservative Free Church of Scotland viewed Americans as shockingly individualistic and conservative. In fact, the Scots are quite socialist by our standards!

Latin America is no different. While one must be careful not to paint such a large and diverse part of the world with a broad brush, committed Christians there express differing political views. For instance, the Christian Democratic Party in Chile is a valid political option for many believers who want to bridge capitalism and communism. In Mexico, the most recent presidential election fielded four registered candidates with diverse political stances. In fact, the growth of liberation theology in Latin America can be viewed, in some sense, as a reaction to American corporate capitalism and Western colonialism. In fact, one has a difficult time reading the "classic" Liberation Theology works without walking away with a clear view of humanity, God, sin and Christ, regardless of how one views the political and eschatological ramifications of these works.

Because there is not one dominant Christian political view, Christians throughout the world have differing political commitments. Some Christians see no theological reason to be against a single-payer healthcare system in the U.K. or Canada, while others see it as a sign of impending totalitarianism. Some Christians have no problem with a strong state in countries like Mexico, Chile or Scotland, while some U.S. believers proudly assert, "Don't tread on me!"

How does this apply to ministry in a state context? Because Christianity has not established a single political system throughout the world, we have freedom to shed individual ideological commitments and realize they are part of a social context.

Social Context

The phrase "all politics is local" provides a great snapshot for one's own political and social milieu. When we moved back to Oklahoma in 2009, I discovered some interesting politics. My wife and I had spent the previous two years in rural Pennsylvania in a largely blue-collar church. In fact, it seemed like the "sweet spot" of a 50/50 split between Democrats and Republicans. What fascinated me was that some parishioners saw their political choices as local ones. They voted Democratic because they were in a union and believed that party provided the best protection of their local interests.

Fast forward to 2010 in Oklahoma. I remember joking with my wife about the difference between Democrats and Republicans in Pennsylvania and Oklahoma. The Democratic candidate for Oklahoma governor in 2010 would have made a fine Pennsylvania Republican, I said. In fact, we typically say that about most Oklahoma Democrats and the other places we have lived like St. Louis, Missouri and Pennsylvania. Context is key.

Another way to see this is through several "hot button" political issues, like immigration. Oklahoma has a growing Latino population, and immigration policy is at the forefront of many people's minds. Yet historically, immigration legislation, national borders and official languages are relatively new. In fact, the U.S. did not begin to regulate immigration until tens of thousands of Chinese flocked to the American West in the nineteenth century. When approached about this issue, I assert that the biblical teaching of humanity's creation in God's image informs how we treat others regardless of what the laws are, or what we think they should be.

A few other issues stem from culture war tropes. For example, in the Bible Belt, it is not uncommon to hear folks bemoan the disrespect of the Pledge of Allegiance and how important it is to say the Pledge and to include the phrase "under God." But a Christian socialist wrote the Pledge during the late 1800s for the purpose of Americanizing immigrant children. In addition, the phrase "under God" was not in the original version. It was added during the Eisenhower Administration after Dr. George MacPherson Docherty preached a sermon in which he asked for "under God" to be added. The president was in attendance and, according to the story, many legislators heard this and rushed to be the first to write the law.

To minister in a state context, we must realize our political views *have* a context. Much of that is based upon location, background and immediate milieu. We should still derive political views from the Scriptures. Many believe the Bible addresses immigration policy or prayer in schools and even capitalism or socialism. When we look at the Bible as a tool chest to construct a master political ideology, we essentially take God's revelation and say it is not for *all* time, but for *our* time. That line of thinking leads us to look back on history and mock the faulty views that came before us (theological support of racism, "biblical" justification for colonialism, etc.). Tim Keller points out that we must be careful to consider what *our* grandchildren will look back on and ask how we believed certain things. We have to see that only a gospel context can drive us to serve those with political views that differ from our own.

Gospel Context

When the New Testament authors admonished Christians to obey their leaders, pray for those in authority and be good citizens, they were not writing in the context of a democratic republic. They wrote in an agrarian society ruled by emperors. They lived in a time in which social and political rights came from the empire. There was no concept of freedom of speech, and no framework for the free market, yet the New Testament writers tell us something profound – to be good citizens.

Throughout the Scriptures humanity is called to two simple yet very hard tasks: to love God with all your heart, soul, mind and strength and to love your neighbor as yourself. Christianity contends that only one person, Jesus Christ, did this perfectly, and through his life, death and resurrection, we can by faith receive the benefits of keeping the Great Commandment – fellowship with the Triune God. The message of Christianity is greater than the message of any government. When the Apostle Paul wrote that whoever confessed "Jesus is Lord" finds salvation, he also, according to some scholars, made the political statement that Christ is above all empires. To the Philippian Church Paul wrote that "every knee will bow." Even Caesar will bow to King Jesus just as the current living Presidents Carter, Bush, Clinton, Bush and Obama will. Adding to this tension, the Apostle Paul sent greetings to Christians who were in the "household of Caesar."

To minister in the context of the state, we must remember that our own political agendas and empires are temporal, but the power and reign of the living God is forever. We love and serve those who are in government not to score political points, but to demonstrate that we are good citizens with an allegiance to a higher kingdom. To be allied with Christ can make us good Republicans, Democrats or Independents. To be aligned with the Kingdom of God means that we have freedom to participate within our own political systems as they exist in time and space, and to serve those in authority.

The gospel is for anyone. It does not belong to a political party or administration. In order to do nonpartisan ministry in a hyper-partisan world, we must realize where our ultimate allegiance lies – in Christ. Many of our political views and positions are based in our own context and will one day be disproved. But the gospel is greater than personal politics. Because of the gospel, we can create space where Christians of differing political stripes can come together and share a meal to hear the gospel applied to their lives as they serve the citizens of their own locale.

One way to keep this at the forefront is to continually ask: Am I so committed to my political ideology that it spills through my messages and offends someone who opposes my *political* views instead of my gospel views? You see, the gospel is always offensive. Christianity will always be offensive. But, like Paul in Athens, we can minister to the hubs of culture and power and declare that through Christ, life can be found. That is good news for Democrats, Republicans, Socialists and everyone else.

To serve in a post-partisan fashion, we keep the Scriptures at the forefront and ourselves in the background. Personally, I disagree with lots of things that occur in Oklahoma politics. Yet I know I am called to love and serve the capitol at this juncture. I would rather be known as the pastor who came and spoke from the Bible and loved the capitol community than as the pastor who came with his political agenda. By remembering the context in which we serve, we can see some folks hear the gospel for the first time and help others grow in their faith.

CHAPTER 9

PURSUING PEACE AND PROSPERITY

CHARLES M. GARRIOTT

I have traveled to Haiti many times, but this was my first visit to Jérémie, an isolated community in the southwest of the country. The small twin prop plane descended toward the dirt runway just off the Caribbean coast, and we spied green tropical hills dotted with concrete block homes. This thirty-minute flight was a welcome option to a six-hour car ride from Port-au-Prince. As the plane made its final approach, I noticed the designated welcoming party of mules and cows that lined the runway.

I waited for my friends outside the small airport terminal, recalling previous visits before I had met Dony and Louis St. Germain. I had spent my first night near Port-au-Prince sleeping under the stars on a hard concrete roof with only a sheet, a flea-bitten dog nestled at my feet, and the sounds of the witch doctor's ghetto blaster next door. That was some years ago; now I was in Jérémie.

This community of seventy-one thousand souls is often called the city of the poets. It was the site of the 1964 massacre known as the Jérémie Vespers, when the army under the direction of dictator François 'Papa Doc' Duvalier killed 27 citizens one night. Although those long years of turmoil had passed, Haiti still bore the scars of dictatorship and corruption. Dony St. Germain and his wife Sharon had moved into Jérémie, sensing a call to serve these people with the gospel.

I had first met Dony and his younger brother, Louis, in the late 1990s. Born in Haiti, they had learned ministry from their father, who developed extensive ministries throughout the country in the sixties. Both brothers were educated in North America before being ordained in the Presbyterian Church in America. In 1995, they started El Shaddai Ministries International. Since its founding, the ministry has developed church leadership in Haiti, along with establishing eighty-one indigenous churches and thirty-five preaching points. Over a thousand children live in their nine orphanages in Les Cayes, Jérémie, and Gonaïves. They also started forty-one schools (elementary through twelfth grade) and five medical clinics. It is all impressive.

When Dony realized their orphans would have no future after finishing high school, he led the decision to establish the University of Jérémie. After only a couple of years, they have 190 students in programs such as agriculture, law, education, business, language/communication, and theology. Our mutual concern for people in government had brought us together; we wanted to see the gospel impact those in leadership.

They had invited me to take part in a dinner with members of Haiti's legislature, Assemblée Nationale, in 2009. The group of about fourteen represented men from both houses of congress, including the President of the Assembly, Kely Bastien. As the members arrived it was clear that Louis St. Germain had established strong relationships with these guests. The evening included extensive conversation regarding needs that exist within this Caribbean country.

They were familiar concerns: better education, roads, and health care. The unemployment rate in many areas approached 75%.

The government had no ability to institute an economic stimulus package or sweeping reforms. Although their needs are great and resources extremely limited, there was clearly a tone of optimism as these men not only related their concerns, but also their hope for the nation's future. When asked why they appeared to get along so well even though they represented five different political parties, the answer was clear: "We know our concerns will be better addressed if we work together." During the dinner, the three of us shared how the gospel fits and impacts our work. We shared biblical examples of wise leadership, such as how King David not only understood the importance of good governance and national security but also his position before a holy and sovereign God. We talked about the importance of having an awareness of the spiritual dimension to their work as national legislators. Soon after the conversation centered on these spiritual matters, the electricity went out. We were forced to continue in complete darkness until candles could be found. I later reflected how that symbolized our work--we function as ministers in a world of complete darkness. The three of us left the meeting encouraged by the promise for further relationships and ministry with those in the Assemblée Nationale.

After my return to Washington, I had lunch with the Haitian Ambassador to the United States, Raymond Joseph. When I asked for his assessment of Haiti's circumstances and condition, he responded, "The last time the country was doing this well was at the time of their independence from France in 1804." Six months after our lunch, a catastrophic earthquake killed between 230,000–300,000 people, and displaced 1.5 million.

In Jérémie, the three of us reviewed what had taken place in the several years since the earthquake and prayed about the future. Louis shared that he had been appointed as an advisor under the Minister of Interior and Defense to smooth relationships with different municipalities in their region, a position which opened many doors. His visits to Port-au-Prince helped him make many friends with those in the Administration, in addition to his relationships with members of the Assemblée Nationale. Other doors to government were opening as well. But there were troubling issues in the region.

These issues motivated the two brothers to call a meeting in 2012 with fifty-five mayors, numerous commissioners and four representatives from the president. They wanted the attendees to know that they were there to help. Was it possible that the church could better serve them and their communities? The gathering focused on at least two issues: bringing unity to the different camps regarding security, and addressing the environmental problem of deforestation. Agriculturalists from Port-au-Prince shared their concerns via video about the threat of deforestation. Haitians cut down and burn trees to create charcoal to heat ovens for baking and large steam containers for dry cleaning. This is destroying the land. Could propane burners be used instead? How could this be implemented and what would it cost?

The issue of security had been accented for Dony and his wife Sharon a couple of years previously. Exhausted from the myriad demands of relocating from Miami, they decided to drive from Port-au-Prince to Santo Domingo, the other side of the island of Hispaniola, to unwind.

As night fell, less than an hour away from the capital, Dony noticed a car fast approaching from the rear. Immediately it began signaling with its lights to pull over—a standard police procedure. When he stopped, one of the men approached the car and asked Dony for papers proving the car belonged to them. It seemed a legitimate request from the police, but something did not seem right to Dony. When Dony presented the document, the man tore it up and told the St. Germains to exit the car. As they opened the doors, Dony realized that these were four armed thugs intent on carjacking and kidnapping them. As the gunmen began to force Sharon into their car, she asked Dony what was happening. Dony could have responded in a number of ways: "I don't know," or, "Just do what they say and we'll be all right"— anything to keep her calm. But he chose his words carefully. Looking at her intently, he said: "We are being kidnapped!" Sharon needed to hear those exact words. With the few seconds she had to think and respond, her mind raced in one direction. Sharon's father had been kidnapped some years before while living in Jamaica, and after a long time it was presumed that he had been killed. However, the absence of the body haunted the family, leaving them without closure as to what really had taken place. Sharon was not going to let that happen again to her family. If her life was being threatened, and it was, then she would die there, on the side of the highway, so at least her body could be found. Her family would have closure.

She stopped and screamed. Immediately she felt the blunt end of a gun on the back of her head, causing intense pain and throbbing. Her resistance would not be tolerated. It was followed by another blow. Dony's resistance earned the same to the back of his head. However, neither of them was going to get into the car. In the midst of the chaos, they noticed the headlights of two cars approaching. Could this be their chance for freedom? Dony, in his limited Spanish, told the one thug that he was a pastor and that they should take the car and all of its possessions, but leave them alone. Without hesitation the leader ordered the other three to get in their car, and sped off in the St. Germain's car with all their belongings. As quickly as it had started, it was over. They were somewhat injured, but they were both alive and free.

This horrific experience was one of the reasons Dony was concerned about crime in their area. Only one road connects Jérémie to the next few towns, so when a crime is committed, the thugs have only one route of escape. It would take little organization to create a system to apprehend the thieves in the next few towns and lower the crime threat.

Other concerns were shared in the meeting as well, and the attendees understood that they were not going to resolve all the issues immediately. But it was a start. The day included lunch, Q & A session, and prayer. Four more meetings of a similar nature have been held since then, resulting in ongoing relationships with various government officials.

The St. Germains are examples of what Jeremiah 29 spoke about in the seventh century BC.

> This is what the LORD Almighty, the God of Israel, says to all those I carried into exile from Jerusalem to Babylon: "Build houses and settle down; plant gardens and eat what they produce. Marry and have sons and daughters; find wives for your sons and give your daughters in marriage, so that they too may have sons and daughters. Increase in number there; do not decrease. Also, seek the peace and prosperity of the city to which I have carried you into exile. Pray to the LORD for it, because if it prospers, you too will prosper". (v. 4-7)

Haiti is changing. There is a sense that under President Michel Martelly the country will continue to know stability. There are new opportunities for economic growth and educational development. In the northern region, resorts and hotels are being established to bolster tourism and employment. But what Haiti really needs is an understanding of the gospel. That message needs to penetrate the hearts of those who live there. God is using the St. Germains to impact not only the people at large with the message of Christ, but especially those in government.

"The question is, 'Can and will the church make a difference? But the prior question is, 'What can and should the church do?' This raises the issue of how the church anywhere should relate to the socio-political issues raised by the various contexts in which it lives."

—Michael Cassidy, Pietermaritzburg,
South Africa 1988

"It is hoped and believed that the Lord has raised you up to the good of His church and for the good of the nation."

—John Newton to William Wilberforce,
December 7, 1785

CHAPTER 10

CHRISTIAN LEADERSHIP IN WASHINGTON: AFTERTHOUGHTS

STEVEN PRESTON

Christians seek leadership positions in Washington for many reasons:

- We come to serve the needy.
- We come to advance policies that enable our countrymen to flourish and to create.
- We come to protect our basic liberties, like freedom of religion, and to fight for justice.
- We come to ensure that our government is an accountable, transparent steward of the mandate it has.

And when we come, we do so with the confidence that we are called to serve. And if our hearts are pure in seeking that call, our mission is good, and it is of God.

My trip to Washington was unlikely. God's pull and providence were undeniable, however, as my wife, Molly, and I considered why God might be calling us there.

In 2005, I was the executive vice president at a large company called ServiceMaster. There was a clear, promising path forward for me at the company. We were blessed financially, my children were flourishing, we were comfortably entrenched in our community, and a church plant that Molly and I had helped nurture for years had finally been launched and was taking hold. Our roots were deep.

But I felt restless. After I prayed for God's direction over time, a variety of compelling professional opportunities began to come my way. Most of them would take me a good step forward in business. Some provided an intriguing career segue into ministry. But none moved my heart. It was as if God were saying, "I am going to show you everything you could want so you can see it and touch it--and say no to it. You will see it for what it is and for what it isn't."

During that time I also had an opportunity to talk with people in the Bush administration about a presidential appointment in the federal government. After several months of discussions and interviews in Washington, Molly and I felt clarity and conviction that this was God's plan for us. I had been offered a significant opportunity that was meaningful and relevant, but not terribly risky—one that I was willing to take.

But a turn of events would take us to a very different place. About two weeks before the president was to nominate me, I received a call from the White House asking if I would consider a different job that was described as "important to the president," and that the White House considered a "higher calling." As a Christian seeking to take the next step in God's plan for my life, the word choice seemed providential.

I was asked to candidate for the role of administrator of the U.S. Small Business Administration (SBA). Most people associate the

SBA with financial services and other programs to support small businesses. Helping entrepreneurs get off the ground and be successful hardly seems like a controversial assignment. However, the SBA is also the arm of the federal government that provides loans to both homeowners and small business owners to help them rebuild their homes and businesses after the destructive effects of natural disasters.

It was 2006, just months after Hurricane Katrina had devastated New Orleans, and the agency was in the center of the Katrina debacle. Its disaster loan program was the primary source of federal support for Americans trying to rebuild their homes and businesses in the Gulf. Without SBA capital flowing, people simply could not put their lives back together. Because of the staggering demand, the SBA lending operations had nearly collapsed. The agency had a huge, intractable backlog of undisbursed disaster loans, the problem was building every day, and it continued to do so through my confirmation. Political leaders and media across the country were lambasting its performance, and the head of the agency, in particular, had come under tremendous attack. To top things off, the agency had the lowest employee morale of the 31 largest federal agencies. Low morale can be particularly lethal in an organization where the provision of service is entirely dependent on its people.

Within a very short time, what had seemed like a clear path to Washington became a struggle that made me look very hard at my motives, my purpose, and God's plans for my life.

The more I learned about the role, the more troubled I became. My joy in moving ahead had dissipated, and a cloud had emerged over my decision. I had never been a terribly public person, and the risk of failure was very real. Moreover, many people whom I trusted counseled me to decline the opportunity, because failure would have such strong negative consequences for my future, and the other opportunities before me were so compelling.

But God had shown me many times that service is not about self, and that in seeking to save my own life, I lose the very life that God seeks to give me. I could see that the opportunity to make an impact, and the opportunity to glorify God in the process, could be tremendous. I took the job and charged ahead.

Our journey was blessed with memorable family experiences, shared victories with a terrific team, and an ongoing affirmation of my call. At SBA, we dramatically accelerated the disbursement of disaster loans following a complete operational redesign. Within a few months, we had cleared out the backlogs and had put $6 billion into the hands of homeowners and small businesses to rebuild their lives. We also engineered marked improvements in our other programs, received growing recognition of our successes in the media and in Congress, and, very importantly, enjoyed a surge in employee morale.

After two unrelenting years full of Congressional hearings, operational restructurings, media exposure and, most importantly, success for Americans, a similar call came to me again. It was early 2008 and the country was in the midst of a burgeoning financial crisis. Bear Stearns had collapsed. Many of the country's largest financial institutions were scrambling to raise capital. Banks were pulling out of the lending business rapidly. The housing market was at the center of the meltdown, as skyrocketing delinquencies in subprime loans and resulting home foreclosures destabilized the financial markets.

On April 1, 2008, I received a call from the White House asking me to candidate for the position of Secretary of Housing and Urban Development (HUD)—and, no, it wasn't an April fool's joke. HUD typically was an agency in the background, dealing with important issues, but generally out of the public eye.

Because the housing and mortgage markets were squarely in the center of the growing crisis, HUD's federal housing assistance programs like FHA were growing exponentially, and HUD would be in the middle of the most hotly debated issues in Congress.

In addition, the agency was under a dark cloud as the outgoing HUD secretary had left under the specter of an investigation into his activities by the Inspector General and potentially other authorities. He would eventually be cleared of any wrongdoing.

The next 18 days were a blur of White House interviews, FBI background investigations, policy briefings, and outreach preparations. I was told that no one in memory had gone through a Cabinet selection process at such an accelerated pace.

So, on April 18th, I found myself walking with President George W. Bush from the Oval Office across the small hallway into the Roosevelt Room, where he would announce my nomination to the public. The Roosevelt Room was normally just a large working conference room where many of the West Wing meetings occurred. As I walked in, I could see that the room had been transformed for the event. Boom mikes hovered over the heads of my wife and children who sat in the front, backed by a crush of cameras just behind the small audience. With every gesture of the president, a burst of clicking cameras could be heard.

The president's remarks were gracious and deeply humbling as he elaborated the character, accomplishments and the qualifications I brought to the role. His words were especially meaningful to me because of the deep respect I held for him as a man of conviction and purpose, driven by a clear set of principles he sought to uphold. I would later see firsthand that in the midst of the financial crisis, he was committed to making tough decisions to put the country on solid footing so that his successor would not have to.

After the president's remarks, we exited the room. As we reentered the Oval Office, he said, sort of over his shoulder, "It is a great day for your family." Then he looked me sternly in the eye and said, "And it's a great day for the country." He then took my talking points from me and wrote on them, "Thank you for serving. George W.

Bush." Although the frenzy of the prior three weeks had reached a culmination that morning, in that moment the swirl of events came to an abrupt stop as my purpose crystallized. It was all clear.

When in Washington, it wasn't difficult to keep a sense of mission top-of-mind. The situations were intensely charged. I knew why I was there, I knew what I had to do, and I knew who I had to be in the middle of it. Paul's exhortation in Philippians 1:27 (NIV), "Whatever happens, conduct yourselves in a manner worthy of the gospel of Christ," was always before me as a guiding principle.

The setting and the circumstances were overwhelming. I knew the gravity, the scale and the public nature of the issues. I also knew my own limitations and shortcomings and knew what public failure could feel like. I certainly had seen other administration officials flayed after difficult tenures. But I also knew that I had been chosen for a reason, and that I had been called upon by the president to be someone in that place, at that time, whatever it took. I owned it. I was deeply honored.

I also found that despite my resoluteness in stepping forward to serve and the clarity of vision God had given me for my roles, I didn't always lead out of the strength he offered in that call. All too often, the constant onslaught of decisions, conflicts, and demands led me to grab the reins tighter, rather than handing them over to the one whose purpose I was there to serve. At the very time God could have been extending his grace to me in the battle, I put myself out there on my own. All too often the yoke was not easy, the living waters ran dry, and life in the Spirit became more academic than actual.

The Road Is Rough: Leaders Need God's Strength to Get the Job Done

Not long after my nomination, I realized that a core of people in politics, the media and special interest groups was aligned to engineer my failure, or the perception thereof, before I ever set foot into Washington. My winning or losing meant political victories or failures for the broader cause, because I had been appointed by the president. Within days of a public announcement, false stories and arguments against my confirmation began to circulate, which was astonishing to me since there was virtually no information about me in the public domain, other than the scant information that had been reported in ServiceMaster's SEC filings. Moreover, I was troubled that a completely unsubstantiated narrative could be advanced in the media. It would, however, be a valuable step in steeling my wife and me for what was ahead. I would later learn that the spread of such misinformation was a common occurrence among political opponents and a media aligned against the president. After our reforms had begun to take hold, a well-known reporter from a large national newspaper was preparing to write a well-researched profile article on me, informed by interviews with notable political and community leaders, many of whom were among the president's most ardent critics. After weeks of research and extensive interviews, the reporter's editor promptly pulled the piece when it turned out that they had been unable to develop a negative story line on me.

In addition to those external pressures, there were the practical obstacles to advancing progress—operational inefficiencies, bureaucratic immobility, and labyrinthine rules and regulations which needed to be maneuvered deftly before anything could be accomplished. Even though one may have clear and noble goals, the snares and entanglements can seem inexhaustible and insurmountable.

Our work on the Katrina issues at the SBA was a perfect example. I was confirmed ten months after the storm, and the backlogs were just getting worse. The more I dug into the issues, the clearer it became that our most basic operational processes were designed in a way that led to errors, lost documents, poor support for victims and desperate levels of inefficiency. None of this was based on a lack of concern or commitment by federal workers. On the contrary, these people cared deeply, worked tirelessly, and desperately wanted to help. Nothing had been set up to help them succeed. Figuring out how to restructure workflows, job functions, customer support, performance tracking, and so on, would be a massive undertaking, and there was little time and little expertise to set the agency on the right course. The path ahead was further complicated by complex contracting regulations which made it difficult to bring in expert support, by antiquated technologies, and by excessive Congressional "oversight," resulting in incessant hearings.

Leaders Need God's Presence to Serve as His Witnesses

Political leaders are exposed to public scrutiny every day. I had 20 congressional hearings in 15 months, often as the sole testifier. Some were perfunctory. Some were important for Congress in performing its essential oversight function of the executive branch. Most, however, were politically motivated by legislators seeking to win political points at my expense, often accentuated by the presence of television cameras. I worked hard to be unassailable with respect to my knowledge of issues, the logic of and motives for my actions, and the honesty of my concerns. My approach and my words mattered both to convey competency in the issues being addressed and also to convey respect toward those people to whom I could just as easily have shown disdain.

The agencies in which I served helped hundreds of thousands of citizens, often during their most desperate time of need. Our citizens needed to see that I came with a heart to serve, and that nothing about my commitment to them was diminished by political motives. One way we did that at SBA was in providing people greater care in the process of receiving disaster aid. In the prevailing system, disaster victims sent extensive documentation required for a disaster loan to a large processing center where their materials were often lost, and they had little visibility into the status of their applications for aid. Questions were directed to our call center, which was often unable to provide some of the most basic support because they didn't have the tools, insight or understanding of the cases to support the disaster victims. We redesigned the entire operational structure to provide each loan applicant with a dedicated, accountable customer service representative with a direct phone number, supported by legal and other resources. By doing so, we accelerated the resolution of issues, improved the quality, and extended personal compassion to disaster victims through caring support.

Finally, I was the leadership face to a large workforce for whom I had a particularly strong affection. There is something special about leading a service organization where people come to work every day to help others. When they have the tools, the training and the support to deliver that assistance with excellence, they can be successful and find joy in the process. When that isn't the case, it brings frustration and can cause people to detach from the mission. I had led agencies where the workforce was often dejected and had at times become disconnected from the mission.

I wanted to make sure the employees understood that I was committed to helping them be excellent, so that our service to people in need would be excellent. On the one hand, I tried to do so by driving a rigorous agenda to fix problems and improve the service levels. However, I also knew that I had a platform to try to inspire the workforce, tying the purpose for operational initiatives to the greater mission. In doing so, I often invoked language that reinforced our mission, focused on those in need, and referenced scripture. Although doing so was a fundamental element of my leadership style, I often wondered how it connected with people. I wanted people to see that my convictions came from a purpose that was bigger than I was. I also wanted to encourage our team to see their work as a mission. One of my most gratifying moments in Washington was when a federal employee grabbed my hand to shake it and said, "You're a believer, aren't you." I was humbled and gratified, but also convicted in the knowledge that often, my actions would not have led others to the same observation.

Finding Joy in the Journey: Leaders Need God's Fellowship to Thrive

As I considered taking that first step forward to serve in Washington, Exodus 33 helped me establish the right frame of mind:

> Moses said to the Lord, "You have been telling me, 'Lead these people,' but you have not let me know whom you will send with me. You have said, 'I know you by name, and you have found favor with me.' If you are pleased with me, teach me your ways so that I may know you, and continue to find favor with you. Remember that this nation is your people."
>
> The Lord replied "My Presence will go with you, and I will give you rest."
>
> Then Moses said to him, "If your Presence does not go with us, do not send us up from here. How will anyone know that you are pleased with me and with your people unless you go with us? What else will distinguish me and your people from all the other people on the face of the earth?" (verses 12-16)

Moses accepted the call from God, knowing that it was central to God's plan for his people. It was a huge job, and it mattered. But he did not accept that call without pleading with God for what he needed and what he desired in God along the way. He wanted to know God better. He wanted to ensure that God's presence was with him so that others would see God through him. And finally, he wanted to see God and experience him on a powerful level.

My decision to go to Washington was ultimately about joy and peace, knowing that outside of God's plan I would have neither. I knew that within his plan, I would be closest to becoming the person he created me to be. That is why it is so ironic that I sometimes allowed that calling to pull me away from him, thereby thwarting its foundational value.

Having a real, dynamic relationship with God provides us clarity and fortifies our resolve. It puts us 'in' God and God 'in' us. It infuses our daily walk with the peace, joy and strength of the Spirit every day, despite the challenges. The issue isn't just becoming rejuvenated in God's rest to then be depleted along the way. It is about living in the joy and energy of the race. It's the runner's high. I am reminded of the Eric Liddell quote in *Chariots of Fire* describing his love of running: "I believe God made me for a purpose, but he also made me fast. And when I run I feel His pleasure." In my own meager way, I get that. When I was serving in Washington, I felt that. Despite the challenges, the best I had to give came out of me—as a leader, as a technical practitioner, and as a caring believer. It all worked, when I was letting the Spirit work through me, and it was there that I found joy.

Targeted Ministry

As lofty as our motives may be, our willingness to enter the political fray is only the first step in a demanding journey that requires a living and enabling faith if we are going to have the strength to get the job done, serve as an effective witness, and thrive in the faith along the way. The church or other targeted ministries can play a valuable, supportive role in this journey.

In other words, though the mission be clear, the sense of calling strong, and the foundation in faith rock-solid, taking that step forward in obedience is only the first step. The pursuit of that mission needs to be of God every day. When we fail to lean on God and live in his Spirit, we can begin to lose the sense of connection to his calling and the power of pursuing it through him. No one's faith walk is a straight line. We often forget whom we are serving. And, we can make our mission more about us than about God. As a result, no matter how much we taste that sense of calling initially, it can fade with each day that we walk further onward. Although this condition is not unique to political leaders, its effect on them has unique manifestations and should be understood by the church as it seeks to minister to them.

A political leader is out front every day. People dissect your words, study your actions, find meaning in your gestures, and ultimately, see who you are at your core. In those circumstances, there are many opportunities to stand tall before others. There are also many opportunities to devolve into the other man's game, using the same tactics.

Although the reasons for ministering to political leaders in Washington are clear, there are obstacles to advancing such a ministry—some are practical, but others are based on a lack of understanding.

Relationships with leaders in Washington can be difficult to cultivate. There is no time. Travel and external obligations are excessive, the workload can be overwhelming, and time with family is precious. In addition, it can be hard to get through to them because of the tight perimeter around them.

In addition, leaders are formidable people with formidable roles. People call them by their titles, not their names. It is hard to perceive a need, sense an openness, or believe one has permission to reach out. It can seem uncomfortable or inappropriate. I will never forget having the head of my children's school hint that he wanted me to join the school's board before he was very familiar with my role. When my HUD nomination hit the press, he jokingly apologized for asking me to join a "rinky-dink" board when I was in such a big job. He was embarrassed he had asked. I felt chagrined that my job somehow implied that I wouldn't be willing to serve. The truth was that although I didn't have time to serve and ethics rules would have prohibited it, there was nothing "rinky-dink" about that request.

Finally, the job can make leaders seem distant. They have boundaries and are often guarded, as a protective mechanism. They come to have difficulty trusting others, and they have tough exteriors as they steel themselves to deal with the challenges. As a result, they often have few confidants, and it may be difficult to break through to reach them on issues that are among the most personal they face.

I think all of us have to start with a certainty that, irrespective of what that calling is, our highest and best purpose in this life is to commit ourselves to a relationship with God, and out of that relationship, to pursue with a passionate sense of mission his calling for our lives, whether it is in ministry, in business, or in being a great neighbor.

I can't help but think about John 17, where Jesus prays for himself, for his disciples, and ultimately for all believers, just before he is arrested. The passage gives us a beautiful picture of the relationship he yearns to have with us and the glory that comes to us and to God through that relationship. Jesus prays, "...that all of them may be one, Father, just as you are in me and I am in you. May they also be in us…" (verse 21). And then later, "I will make you known to them, and will continue to make you known in order that the love you have for me will be in them and that I myself will be in them" (verse 26). Certainly, for me, the relationship with God was the one thing that was constantly assailed in Washington.

What does all of this mean? The church needs to be bold in breaking through; bold in seeking to understand the need; and bold in ministering to that need. Know that the church is needed: the demands are overwhelming, and these leaders need to be supported. Don't be fooled by their success or their stature—the need is there.

Finally, be confident that the value to our country is great. Leadership in government affects the lives of millions of people and continues to do so over the years. Godly leadership matters and can have an enormous impact for good, whether in government, the ministry, or the private sector.

ACKNOWLEDGEMENTS

Some years ago a symposium was held at Park Cities Presbyterian Church in Dallas, Texas for the purpose of reflecting on the mission of the church to those in places of leadership both nationally and internationally. A part of the conversation centered on the need to have a written expression of what it would look like to engage leaders, and those who serve them, with the gospel. Such encouragement from these friends is greatly appreciated and is the reason for this book.

Each contributor listed in the table of contents composed his chapter without knowing the exact context of the work. Their compositions were based on their experience and their guiding principles from the perspective of the gospel as revealed in the Old and New Testaments. They willingly dedicated their valuable time to this book, and are kind, gracious servants of the one true King. I am humbled by their friendship and love.

Any written work such as this would not be possible unless two very good friends, Maria Garriott and Barbara Harley, were willing to take out their editing tools and diligently apply them to every inch of the manuscript. Thank you both so very much. I would never want to do such a project without you.

My work with Ministry to State is under the auspices of Mission to North America (MNA), Presbyterian Church in America. The MNA leadership, Jim Bland and Fred Marsh, and their staff in Atlanta make it possible for me to engage in my work. Their support is invaluable.

The Ministry to State team in Washington, Martha Iverson Robinson, Eric Tracy and my wife Debby, spent a great deal of time helping me sort out the various concepts of the manuscript in the beginning months. Your effort, encouragement and work are more than noted. Thank you.

ENDNOTES

Chapter 1 Calling

1. I first met Jake Mabaso and his wife Anna in May of 1991 at their home in Orlando, Soweto (South West Township). Jake was a minister in the Church of England of South Africa, and had been referred to me by Rev. Martin Morrison. They both represented a theologically conservative church in comparison to the Church of the Province. During the sabbatical our two families came together a number of times at their home and church and at our place in Blairgowie, in the northern suburbs of Johannesburg. Our background and lives were very different. Our friendship was an important part of what God was teaching the Garriotts. Their oldest daughter Priscilla, who at the time of our sabbatical lived in New York, eventually lived with us in Oklahoma City and attended the University of Central Oklahoma.

2. Michael Cassidy, *The Passing Summer: A South African's Response to White Fear, Black Anger, and the Politics of Love* (Regal Books/African Enterprise, A Division of GL Publications, 1989), p. 353.

3. Paul Johnson, *Modern Times*: *The World from the Twenties to the Nineties* (Harper Collins Publishers, 1991), 783.

4. Ibid., p. 784.

5. Ibid. 2, p. 352,353.

6. Ibid. 2, p. 108 – 127.

7. The term "smart ministry" has nothing to do with the intellectual ability of the one in ministry, or I would be disqualified. It is a term coined from the concept of a Smart Bomb (a precision-guided munition designed to achieve greater accuracy).

8. See Barna Group, *Number of Unchurched Adults Has Doubled Since 1991* https://www.barna.org/barna-update/article/5-barna-update/140-number-of-unchurched-adults-has-nearly-doubled-since-199#.UzNB2I-WjP9s.

Chapter 5 God, Give Me the Humility of Jesus

9. C.S. Lewis, *George MacDonald, An Anthology: 365 Readings* (Harper-Collins, 2009).

10. Henri Nouwen, *The Way of the Heart* (Ballentine Books, 2003), 11. Italics and bold added.

11. Tim Keller, *Encounters with Jesus* (Dutton, 2013).

12. General Colin Powell, *A Leadership Primer* http://www.slideshare.net/duncan2458/colin-powell-a-leadership-primer-5955039.

13. Westminster Larger Catechism, revised.

14. Ibid.

15. C.S. Lewis, *The Great Divorce* (HarperOne, 2009).

Chapter 7 Introduction to Christian Social Ethics

16. St. Augustine, *The City of God.*

17. J. Douma, *The Ten Commandments* (P & R Publishing, 1996), p. 185, 189.

18. St. John of Damascus, *Apology Against the Iconoclasts.*

19. Edmund P. Clowney, *Christian Scholar's Review* (Fall 1970), 15.

20. Nicholas Wolterstorff in *Toward an Evangelical Public Policy*, ed. Ronald J. Sider and Diane Knippers (Baker, 2005), 140-62.

21. Geerhardus Vos, *The Teaching of Jesus Concerning the Kingdom and the Church.*

22. Skillen and McCarthy in *Political Order and the Plural Structure of Society* (Eerdman's, 1991).

23. John Calvin to Jeanne d'Albret, January 20, 1563.

24. Jeanne d'Albret, Preamble to Ecclesiastical Ordinances (November 1571).

25. Lamin Sanneh in *Faith and Power* (Wipf & Stock Pub., 1998).

26. Paul Marshall, *Radical Islam's Rules* (Rowman & Littlefield, 2005).

27. Constitution of the United States, Article VI, ratified 1789.

28. First Amendment, ratified 1792.

29. The 1788 Form of Government and Discipline.

30. John Courtney Murray, *We Hold These Truths: Catholic Reflections on the American Proposition* (Sheed & Ward, 1960).

31. Ibid.

32. William Lee Miller, *The Protestant and Politics* (Westminster Press, 1958), 23.

33. Jean Bethke Elshtain, "Religion and American Democracy," in *Public Morality, Civic Virtue, and the Problem of Modern Liberalism* (Eerdmans, 2000), 14-23.

34. Michael J. Perry, *Under God? Religious Faith and Liberal Democracy* (CUP, 2003), 39.

35. Martin Franzmann, "For Charity Toward Men in Office," *Pray for Joy* (Concordia, 1970).

ABOUT THE AUTHORS

Steve Bostrom is a Colorado native, born and raised in Colorado Springs. Captured by the gospel at age seven, he is still gladly held in its thrall. He and his wife, Via, have eight children and eight grandchildren. Steve has planted two churches, pastored two more and started an adoption agency. He serves as pastor at large in Helena, Montana, the capital.

Charles Garriott was born in Baltimore, Maryland, and educated in his hometown and in St. Louis, Missouri. For over twenty years he pastored in Oklahoma City, Oklahoma. He develops ministry to those in government in Washington, D.C., state, and international capitals, under the auspices of Mission to North America, Presbyterian Church in America. He has authored *Work Excellence: A Biblical Perspective of Work* and *Obama Prayer: Prayers for the 44th President.* He lives with his wife Debby in the District of Columbia. They have four children and four grandchildren.

Bobby Griffith is one of the pastors and church planters of City Presbyterian in Oklahoma City. He possesses masters' degrees from

Covenant Theological Seminary, West Virginia University and is completing a doctorate from the University of Oklahoma. He lives in the OKC metro area with his wife and their son, and serves on the board of a local foster care agency.

Dr. David Clyde Jones is professor emeritus of systematic theology and ethics at Covenant Theological Seminary. After serving for two years as a missionary-pastor on Grand Cayman Island in the West Indies, Dr. Jones joined the Seminary faculty in 1967. His special interest, Christian ethics, is reflected in his publications and service on national church committees dealing with subjects such as nuclear war, medical ethics, divorce, and abortion. Dr. Jones's sensitivity to these and other issues which directly affect the church have made his classes a special mixture of practical and theoretical material. He is the author of *Biblical Christian Ethics*. Dr. Jones retired in 2007, but continues to be available for occasional teaching at the seminary and elsewhere, along with his ongoing ministry of writing and consulting on various ethical issues. Dr. Jones and his wife have two sons and six grandchildren.

Glenn Parkinson, a native of Annapolis, Maryland, came to Christ out of atheism as a college student. He studied at Gordon-Conwell and Westminster seminaries. A pastor for almost four decades in what is now the Presbyterian Church in America, Dr. Parkinson has served 33 years at Severna Park Evangelical Presbyterian Church in Severna Park, Maryland. Glenn is blessed with a wife of 39 years, one daughter, two grandsons, and a cat.

Steven C. Preston has headed two federal agencies, serving on the Cabinet of George W. Bush, first as the Administrator of the U.S. Small Business Administration (2006-2008) and later as the Secretary of the U.S. Department of Housing and Urban Development (2008-2009). He has also had an extensive private sector career as a CEO, a CFO and an investment banker.

Dr. Harry L. Reeder, III, is the senior pastor at Briarwood Presbyterian Church in Birmingham, Alabama. Increasingly his time outside the pulpit is spent doing conferences on Christian manhood and effective leadership. Additionally Dr. Reeder is devoted to the ministry of church revitalization and leads a number of seminars each year both nationally and internationally. He authored *The Leadership Dynamic* and *From Embers to a Flame* and is under contract for several more books.

Dr. Rodney Wood has served in ministry to the Louisiana State Senate and House of Representatives since 1993. Since the year 2000, he has led the Louisiana Legislators' Bible Study/Prayer Breakfast, which meets weekly during the legislative session. Dr. Wood has also served in pastoral ministry in the U.S. and has done interim pastoral work in the UK and Ethiopia. He has preached and taught in many countries in Europe, Asia, and Africa. He is a preaching facilitator with Langham Partnership International. Rodney and his wife Becky live in Baton Rouge, and have three married adult sons, seven grandchildren, and a daughter and granddaughter with the Lord.